THE
KERBER'S
FARM
COOKBOOK

THE
KERBER'S
FARM
COOKBOOK

A Year's Worth of Seasonal
Country Cooking

NICK VOULGARIS III

Photography by
LINDSAY MORRIS

Illustrations by
ROBIN DIAMOND

RIZZOLI
NEW YORK

New York Paris London Milan

First published in the
United States of America in 2019 by
Rizzoli International Publications, Inc.
300 Park Avenue South
New York, NY 10010
www.rizzoliusa.com

All interior and cover photographs © Lindsay Morris
except for the following:
Courtesy of Arthur Kerber: pp. 14, 16 (both), and 17.
Courtesy of Charlie McMillen: p. 26 (top right).
Courtesy of Lisle Richards: p. 27.
© Shopkeep, Inc.: pp. 120 (bottom left), 126,
162 (top left and middle left), 198, and back cover
(jam in box).
© Shutterstock.com/Titus Group: pp. 59, 101, 155, and
191 (background image).
Courtesy of Nick Voulgaris: pp. 2–3, 8–9, 26 (all
except top right), 31 (bottom left), 33, 34, 35, 37,
53, 58, 69 (all except top left and bottom left), 76
(bottom right), 82 (bottom left), 89, 109 (top and
middle left), 118–119, 120 (bottom right), 122 (both),
125 (top right), 139, 154, 160–161, 162 (top right), 166
(top right and bottom left), 177 (all except bottom
right), 190, 199, 202, 203 (all except top left), front
cover (Nick), and back cover (eggs and butterfly).
© Doug Young: pp. 4, 15, 47, 69 (bottom right), 76
(bottom left), 77, 79, 80, 82 (top and bottom right),
83, 86, 106, 111, 120 (top right), 203 (top left), and
front cover (herbs and corn).

Publisher: Charles Miers
Associate Publisher: James Muschett
Managing Editor: Lynn Scrabis
Editor: Candice Fehrman
Design: Susi Oberhelman
Illustrator: Robin Diamond

Printed in China

2019 2020 2021 2022 / 10 9 8 7 6 5 4 3 2 1

ISBN-13: 978-1-59962-154-8
Library of Congress Catalog Control Number:
2019938196

Visit us online:
Facebook.com/RizzoliNewYork
Twitter: @Rizzoli_Books
Instagram.com/RizzoliBooks
Pinterest.com/RizzoliBooks
Youtube.com/user/RizzoliNY
Issuu.com/Rizzoli

CONTENTS

⇥ INTRODUCTION ⇤

I REALLY DON'T REMEMBER THE EXACT MOMENT WHEN THE IDEA of buying Kerber's Farm popped into my mind. I think it was probably during the summer of 2009, as I remember there was a warm breeze coming through the car windows when I drove by the abandoned property. Kerber's was a local treasure situated on a cute country road in Huntington, Long Island, and I wondered why it had closed.

Kerber's was a fixture during my childhood. The farm and its country store were well loved by the local community and surrounding neighborhoods. Back then, Kerber's was the go-to place for eggs, chickens, homemade pies, fresh baked goods, and homegrown

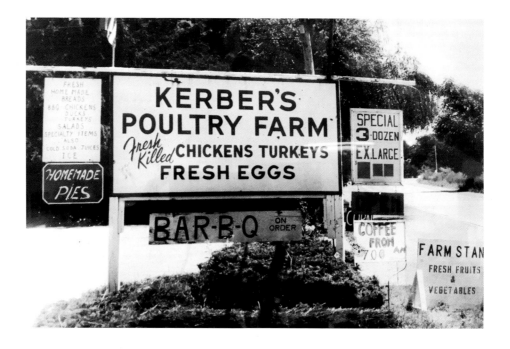

ABOVE: The roadside sign for Kerber's Farm during the 1960s, when it was one of Long Island's leading poultry farms. OPPOSITE: Kerber's Farm owner Nick Voulgaris with his English Labrador, Charlie.

vegetables. Kerber's Farm exuded that small-town charm one would expect from a roadside farm stand set in a Norman Rockwell painting. President Dwight Eisenhower was even a Kerber's customer when he was the head of Columbia University in New York City.

I can still remember going there with my mom during the 1980s to shop for local provisions. When I obtained my learner's permit, Kerber's was the first place I was allowed to drive to alone, so I routinely offered to go there and shop for my mom—anything for a chance to drive the car. Although I was only 17 at the time and had very little life experience, I could already sense there was something nostalgic and old-fashioned about Kerber's Farm, and that appealed to me. As I pulled into the store, the gravel in the parking lot made a pleasant clicking sound as it was thrown up into the wheel wells of the car. Kerber's was also surrounded by 350 acres of preserved farmland, which further enhanced the feeling of being in another world, far removed from the hustle and bustle of nearby downtown Huntington.

Paul Kerber and his wife Evelyn started the farm during the 1940s when Paul taught at Farmingdale State College. He also taught farming techniques to the Women's Army Auxiliary Corps during World War II so the women could grow food on Long Island while their spouses were serving overseas.

ABOVE, LEFT: Evelyn Kerber with her sons, Arthur (left) and Peter (right), and the children's uncle George (middle) in 1949. ABOVE, RIGHT: Arthur Kerber with turkeys in 1950. OPPOSITE: The original Kerber's store—which still stands today—as seen in 1948, with the family's 1941 Ford Super Deluxe Woody Wagon parked in front.

When the Kerbers purchased the farm, it already had a few chicken coops and barns. Over time, they added a small country store at the foot of the property and a winding gravel driveway that led to several barns and more chicken coops. The family eventually built two small houses where several generations of Kerbers lived. Two of the barns that still remain at Kerber's today were purchased from the nearby property of Otto Kahn and literally dragged along the potato fields to their new home. These barns originally served as barracks to house Civilian Conservation Corps workers during the Depression, but by the 1940s they were no longer in use. Paul purchased the structures at surplus and used them for production facilities and to house his live poultry.

In its heyday, Kerber's Farm had more than 200,000 live chickens, ducks, and turkeys on the property at any given time. The Kerbers sold both chickens and their eggs, and also made an array of specialty food items with the farm's bounty. It was the only farm in the area at the time that sold brown eggs. Although customers were at first skeptical of eggs that were not white, the brown eggs eventually became very popular and are still sold at Kerber's today.

Arthur Kerber, the son of the founder, told me the family used to grow apples, plums, and wild black raspberries on the land to bake fresh pies. His grandmother, Bertha, baked the pies using lard instead of butter, a trend at the time. Evelyn tended the garden and grew peonies and other flowers to sell in the store. Arthur and his brother Peter worked on the farm, cared for the poultry, and also went out to Eatons Neck in Northport to dig for fresh clams—which is why you will find an incredible recipe for clams on the half shell in the summer section of this book.

As far as I can remember, the business operated until the early 2000s, but by then times had changed and things were different. The Kerbers sold the business, and it eventually fell into disrepair and closed.

After passing the shuttered farm for months during the summer of 2009, I finally decided to pull back into that gravel driveway and peer into the windows of the old store. It looked as if someone had just closed up shop yesterday, even though it had been years. I could see the same vintage yellow tile I remembered as a child, and the sloped floors that led to drains for when they slaughtered the chickens. There was still a cash register on the counter, a soda machine, a chicken rotisserie, and empty egg cartons strewn about the floor.

I was in disbelief that this once-iconic store had been shut down and that nobody was trying to save such a special place. There was a "For Sale by Owner" sign posted in the ground. I called and left a voicemail, but it was never returned. Although the asking price was well beyond what I could afford, I still had dreams of bringing the old place back to life.

Over the next few years, every time I drove past Kerber's Farm, I felt obligated to call again. But the result was always the same: I left a message on the answering machine, but nobody called me back. The property seemed forgotten, yet occasionally an older man operated a small farm stand there. He was somehow related to the owners at the time, and I pleaded with him to get them to call me. But all he did was take my business card and tell me he would give it to the owners. They still never called.

Seeing Kerber's abandoned for all of those years was very unsettling. The surrounding area was full of lush farmland that had fortunately been preserved. It had a feeling of what Long Island probably looked like 50 years ago—full of potato fields, small farming operations, and quaint shops. But things were different in the 2000s. Just beyond this little pocket of

OPPOSITE: Mementos from the early days of Kerber's Farm, including Thanksgiving turkey cooking instructions, a Kerber's Farm oven mitt, a Kerber's Farm ashtray (the phone number remains the same today), and a thermometer from the Long Island Cauliflower Association.
FOLLOWING SPREAD: Kerber's Farm owner Nick Voulgaris and his dog Charlie digging for clams and steamers on the shores of Shelter Island, New York (left). Nick and his friends sailing aboard his boat Scout in Sag Harbor, New York (right).

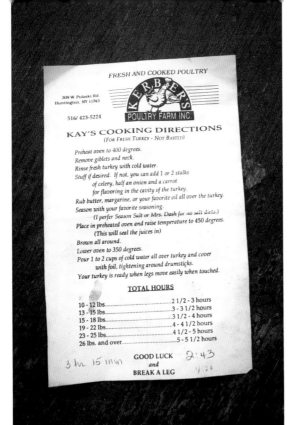

FRESH AND COOKED POULTRY

KERBER'S POULTRY FARM INC.

309 W. Pulaski Rd.
Huntington, NY 11743

516/ 423-5224

KAY'S COOKING DIRECTIONS
(For Fresh Turkey - Not Basted)

Preheat oven to 400 degrees.
Remove giblets and neck.
Rinse fresh turkey with cold water.
Stuff if desired. If not, you can add 1 or 2 stalks
    of celery, half an onion and a carrot
    for flavoring in the cavity of the turkey.
Rub butter, margarine, or your favorite oil all over the turkey.
Season with your favorite seasoning.
    (I perfer Season Salt or Mrs. Dash for no salt diets.)
Place in preheated oven and raise temperature to 450 degrees.
    (This will seal the juices in)
Brown all around.
Lower oven to 350 degrees.
Pour 1 to 2 cups of cold water all over turkey and cover
    with foil, tightening around drumsticks.
Your turkey is ready when legs move easily when touched.

TOTAL HOURS

10 - 12 lbs.	2 1/2 - 3 hours
13 - 15 lbs.	3 - 3 1/2 hours
15 - 18 lbs.	3 1/2 - 4 hours
19 - 22 lbs.	4 - 4 1/2 hours
23 - 25 lbs.	4 1/2 - 5 hours
26 lbs. and over	5 - 5 1/2 hours

GOOD LUCK
and
BREAK A LEG

KERBER'S POULTRY FARMS
"L.I'S. LARGEST PRODUCER OF FRESH GRADE AA EGGS"

309 W. Pulaski Rd., (Near Oakwood Rd.)
Huntington, N. Y. 11743
Phone:
(516) HA 3-5224

KERBER'S POULTRY FARM
FRESH KILLED
CHICKENS   TURKEYS
FRESH EGGS   CHICKEN PARTS
WEST PULASKI RD. - HUNTINGTON, L.I.
HU. 4-5224

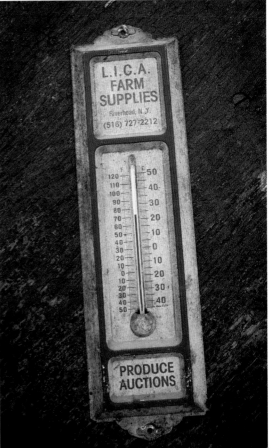

L.I.C.A.
FARM
SUPPLIES
Riverhead, N.Y.
(516) 727-2212

PRODUCE AUCTIONS

heaven that Kerber's was holding on to, only a quarter mile away, stood the realities of urban sprawl. Strip malls, mini-marts, randomly placed parking lots, and other ill-conceived developments dotted every inch of the four-lane Route 25.

By 2012, rumors were circulating that Kerber's was going to be bulldozed to make way for yet another cul-de-sac or row of condominiums. This only exacerbated the sense of urgency I felt to buy the land. To me, the fact that Kerber's Farm was for sale represented an opportunity to not only preserve the property from development, but also revive the legacy that was dear to so many people. But I was still unable to reach the owners.

In the first days of January 2013, I drove by Kerber's once again, just after a fresh blanket of snow had fallen. To my surprise, I noticed a formal real estate broker's sign in the ground. I immediately pulled over and called the broker from my car. She told me the property had been listed only two days earlier. Although I lived in Manhattan, I promptly made an appointment to return the following day to see the property.

Until this point, I had only ever seen what was visible from the street: the store and one small house. During the tour with the broker, I began to understand the breadth of the property. There were seemingly countless rambling structures on the land, including numerous barns, two houses, the retail store, the farm stand, and a 1,500-square-foot enclosed chicken coop. As I calmly walked the property with the broker, I was bursting inside. My mind raced with all of the ideas and potential I saw for the property. I thought about a kitchen to make jam, another to bake pies, a farming educational school, a bed-and-breakfast, and a revamped storefront. I didn't want to share any of these ideas with her out of fear that somebody else would do them. Or was I crazy? Why wasn't anyone else already doing these things?

The new asking price was shockingly 75 percent less than what the owners were previously asking. This made me both excited and scared. Again I wondered why someone else hadn't already made an offer, and if there was something wrong that I was missing. Despite these reservations, I persisted with making an offer that very day. I found out that because of the New Year's holiday and the snowstorm, I was the first person to see the property with the broker, so I didn't want to waste a minute out of concern that somebody else would swoop in and take away my dream.

It was clear to me that the property would not qualify for a traditional commercial mortgage since the business was not operating and the buildings were in very poor condition. And although I saw it as a bit of a Hail Mary, I offered the broker full asking price if I could pay

OPPOSITE: Kerber's organic vegetable garden, with one of the guest cottages in the background.

50 percent down in cash and have the owner hold the mortgage for the remaining balance for five years. I wasn't convinced this offer would be accepted, but it was the only strategy I could come up with that worked for me at the time.

Over the next several days, I flew to Maine to do research for my first book on Hinckley yachts. As I boarded the plane to return home, the broker called and informed me that the owners decided to accept the deal. I was shocked. The first call I made was to my father; I told him, "I am getting into the pie business!" And within a few days, I sold my Apple stock so I could make apple pies.

ABOVE: The Kerber's Farm Land Rover "Millie" offering fresh baked goods, produce, and eggs at Sag Harbor's summer farmers' market. OPPOSITE: Nick Voulgaris in front of one of the original chicken coops that have been restored at Kerber's Farm, which now only raises chickens for fresh eggs. FOLLOWING SPREAD: Nick entertaining friends both at home in New York City and aboard his boat *Scout* in Nantucket, Massachusetts.

SPRING

THE FIRST SIGNS OF SPRING AT KERBER'S FARM ARE USUALLY the stalwart buds that appear on all of the trees and shrubs. This is an exciting time. The break in the weather brings warmer temperatures and plenty of work to be done outside. The birds begin to sing more gleefully once the snow has melted, and a vast sea of yellow fig buttercups pops up in the fields. Outdoor chores include raising baby chicks, tending to the honeybees, planting the garden, and doing repair work on any of the barns that may need attention.

Each spring, we typically get a small batch of baby chicks, which we raise indoors under a warm light before they are allowed to roam around the property or be transferred to one of the chicken coops. When they are just born, we keep them in the corner of the store in a comfy pen. Our customers love seeing them and are enamored by how cute they are. These young chicks will grow up to be the laying hens that provide our farm with fresh eggs. Typically, each bird will lay one egg per day. The young chicks are allowed outside on their own at around five weeks old—or once they have grown the feathers that will help keep them warm. We have several varieties of chickens at Kerber's Farm, including Buckeyes, Rhode Island Reds, Dark Brahmas, and Barred Plymouth Rocks.

Another important part of springtime is tending to our beehives. We carefully check each hive first to be sure they are all still alive. We do sometimes "lose" a hive, which is when the bees leave their hive and do not return, or die due to some unknown reason. Colony collapse disorder, as it is known, is a serious threat to the bee population. The exact cause is still unknown, but researchers believe it can be due to the overuse of pesticides, climate change, mites, disease, or other reasons. We do typically lose a hive or two each year, which we then need to replace. Remarkably, we are able to order a complete package that includes approximately 20,000 worker bees along with one queen. The new set of bees comes in a small, screened cage about the size of a shoebox. The bees are transferred to the wooden hive box, and then they hopefully adapt well and start building honeycomb. Usually by late July we start seeing honey, which we then harvest and jar in our kitchen.

In our garden, we learn with each passing year which plants thrive and which do not. Each spring we plant salvia, snapdragons, zinnias, sunflowers, angelonia, lantana, and marigolds. Our perennials that can endure through the winter include lavender, lemon balm, and sedum. Once in bloom, we sell these items in the store throughout the summer.

The vegetable garden typically includes various types of tomatoes, cucumbers, squash, Black Beauty eggplant, romaine lettuce, pole beans, and celery. Many of these vegetables are started from seeds indoors in March or April and then transferred to the garden around Mother's Day. We also grow a variety of herbs that we use in the kitchen, which can also be dried for later use. These include rosemary, sage, parsley, thyme, basil, cilantro, dill, and mint. Our garden is 100 percent organic, and we do not use pesticides or chemicals of any kind.

We have developed a little ecosystem at Kerber's Farm where the flowers and vegetables are a great food source for the bees and the bees in turn help pollinate the garden. The vegetables, herbs, eggs, and honey that we harvest are either sold at our farm stand or used in the kitchen to make many of the recipes found in this book.

SPRING RECIPES

Coconut Cream Pie

{ MAKES ONE 9-INCH PIE }

This is one of the most popular pies at Kerber's Farm, and it is relatively easy to make. Served chilled, the velvety smooth inside is thick and sweet, with the delightful contrast of small bits of flaky coconut. Not to be confused with coconut custard (which is when the filling is baked in the crust), this recipe makes a coconut pudding and then adds it to the crust after it is baked. Because this pie needs to stay refrigerated, it can be made a day or two in advance.

1½ cups unsweetened coconut milk

1½ cups heavy cream

¾ cup granulated sugar

1½ teaspoons vanilla extract

5 egg yolks

¼ cup cornstarch, sifted

1 tablespoon unsalted butter

2 cups flaked coconut, pulsed until fine in food processor

1 graham cracker crust (see page 90)

2 cups whipped cream (see page 133)

½ cup coconut flakes, toasted on ungreased baking sheet until brown

In a small pot over medium to high heat, combine the coconut milk, cream, sugar, and vanilla. While this is heating, whisk together the egg yolks and cornstarch in a separate bowl. Once the milk mixture comes to a boil, turn off the heat. Take 1 cup of the hot milk mixture from the pot and slowly pour it into the yolk mixture while whisking vigorously.

Next, pour all of the yolk mixture back into the pot and place it on medium heat, whisking until thickened (about 30 seconds to 1 minute), and then immediately remove it from the heat again. Add the butter and coconut flakes, and mix until the butter is completely melted.

Pour the coconut cream into a bowl and place in the fridge until completely cooled, which takes about 3 hours. Once chilled, spread the coconut cream filling into a baked 9-inch graham cracker crust. Using a spatula, cover the pie completely with approximately ½ inch of whipped cream, forming a slight peak in the center. Top with the toasted coconut flakes. Serve or return to the refrigerator.

Lemon Crinkle Cookies

{ MAKES APPROXIMATELY 16 COOKIES }

These zesty cookies are not only bursting with a sweet lemon flavor; they also have a vibrant appearance from the crinkle effect of the bright white powdered sugar juxtaposed with the yellow cookie dough. They are soft and moist, and will hardly last once they are out of the oven.

In a small bowl, combine the flour, salt, baking powder, and baking soda. Whisk thoroughly and set aside.

In a stand mixer fitted with a paddle attachment, combine the butter and sugar. Mix on medium speed until light and fluffy. Add the extracts and eggs to the mixer, scraping down the sides of the bowl with a rubber spatula to ensure even mixing. Add the zest, lemon juice, and food coloring. With the mixer running on low, slowly add the dry ingredients, mixing until just combined. Chill the dough in the fridge for 2 hours or until ready to use.

Preheat the oven to 350°F. Line a baking sheet with parchment paper or grease lightly.

Portion out the dough into balls using a 1½-inch scoop, or scoop by hand, making golf ball–sized balls. Roll each ball in the crystal sugar and then the powdered sugar.

Place the cookies on the prepared baking sheet and bake for 15 to 17 minutes. Let cool to room temperature.

1¾ cups all-purpose flour

¼ teaspoon salt

¼ teaspoon baking powder

¼ teaspoon baking soda

8 tablespoons (1 stick) unsalted butter, softened

1 cup granulated sugar

1 teaspoon vanilla extract

1 teaspoon lemon extract

1 egg

1 egg yolk

2 tablespoons lemon zest

4½ teaspoons lemon juice (from 1 or 2 lemons)

1 teaspoon yellow food coloring

¼ cup crystal sugar, for rolling

¼ cup powdered sugar, for rolling

Lemon Scones

{ MAKES 12 SCONES }

Our scones have become legendary over the past several years, and we make countless varieties using the same basic recipe, with only slight variations for different flavors. Below is the recipe for our lemon scones, with modifications to make blueberry or chocolate chip scones listed on the following page.

FOR THE SCONES:

6 cups all-purpose flour

¼ cup granulated sugar

3 tablespoons baking powder

2 teaspoons salt

2 tablespoons lemon zest

8 tablespoons (1 stick) unsalted butter, cut into ½-inch chunks and chilled

2 cups heavy cream

FOR THE GLAZE:

2 cups powdered sugar

1½ teaspoons lemon zest

2 tablespoons lemon juice (from 2 lemons)

1 tablespoon corn syrup

½ teaspoon vanilla extract

Pinch of salt

SPECIAL EQUIPMENT:

3½-inch biscuit cutter

Preheat the oven to 350°F. Line a baking sheet with parchment paper or grease lightly.

To make the scones, add the flour, sugar, baking powder, salt, and lemon zest to a small bowl. Whisk to combine.

Add the butter to the flour mixture. Using a pastry cutter or your fingers, knead the butter chunks into the flour until they are reduced to pea-sized pieces. Add the heavy cream and mix until just combined.

Place the dough on a lightly floured surface and knead a few times just until the dough is not too wet, taking care not to overknead. Using a rolling pin, roll the dough out to a 1-inch thickness. Dip the biscuit cutter into flour and then cut out the scones, using only an up-and-down motion. Avoid twisting the cutter to get the scones out (this will prevent the scones from rising as high).

Gently lift the scones and place them on the prepared baking sheet. Gently re-roll the dough until all of it is used. Bake the scones for 20 to 25 minutes.

Make the glaze as the scones are baking. In a small bowl, add the powdered sugar, zest, lemon juice, corn syrup, vanilla, and salt. Whisk until mixed well. Once the scones are baked, remove them from the oven and let cool slightly. Cover generously with the glaze while the scones are still warm. Let the glaze set at room temperature.

Scone Variations

To make blueberry scones, add 2 cups of fresh blueberries before adding the cream. For chocolate chip scones, omit the lemon zest and add 2 cups of mini chocolate chips. For a vegan variation, omit the salt and replace the regular butter with a plant-based buttery spread, such as Earth Balance. Replace the cream with full-fat coconut milk.

Deviled Eggs

This is my version of the venerable deviled egg, which I created back when I was
a caterer and served at cocktail parties. Although this dish has certainly
been popular with the old guard since the 1940s, younger folks today wanting
a protein-based snack will also find it appealing. The relish gives the eggs a
slightly sweet taste and helps meld all of the flavors together.

1 dozen eggs

½ cup mayonnaise

2 tablespoons sweet
relish

1 tablespoon unsalted
butter, softened

1 tablespoon Dijon
mustard

1½ teaspoons salt

¾ teaspoon pepper

Gently place the eggs in a saucepan and fill with water
until they are covered by approximately 1 inch. Bring to
a boil over medium-high heat. Once boiling, cover and
continue to cook for approximately 8 minutes.

Immediately drain the eggs and run under cool water
to make removing the shells easy. Once the eggs are
cool, remove the shells and then slice each egg in half
lengthwise and gently remove the egg yolks.

Place the yolks in a bowl and add the remaining
ingredients. Using a mixer or a fork and spoon, combine
the ingredients until they are well blended and a creamy
consistency. Place the yolk mixture in a piping bag and
pipe into each egg half, filling each cavity to slightly
above the surface.

Lemon Chicken Orzo

{ SERVES 4 TO 6 }

This recipe is inspired by the classic Greek lemon chicken soup *avgolemeno*, which I ate as a child in Greek diners around New York City. The soup is filled with chunks of chicken and vegetables, as well as orzo pasta. The delicious broth is hearty with a great lemony flavor, staying true to its name with the zest and juice from a whole lemon.

Preheat the oven to 350°F.

In a small bowl, add the sliced chicken, olive oil, rosemary, brown sugar, pepper, and salt. Mix to coat the chicken. Place the chicken slices on a rimmed baking sheet and bake for 20 minutes or until the chicken is cooked through. Let them cool slightly. Reserve the cooking juices.

In a medium pot, add the chicken juices and place over medium-high heat. Add the onions, carrots, and celery. Sauté for approximately 5 minutes until the onions are translucent and the vegetables are slightly browned.

Add the chicken broth, stirring to incorporate any browned bits at the bottom of the pot. Bring to a boil. Once it boils, reduce the heat to medium and add the lemon zest and juice, parsley, garlic powder, and orzo. Cook until the orzo is tender, approximately 15 minutes, and stir occasionally. While the orzo is cooking, chop the chicken breast into small cubes and add to the soup.

1 pound chicken breast, cut into thin slices

2 tablespoons olive oil

1 tablespoon finely chopped rosemary

1 teaspoon light brown sugar

1 teaspoon pepper

1 teaspoon salt

½ cup diced onion

1 cup diced carrots

½ cup diced celery

8 cups chicken broth

Zest and juice from 1 lemon

1 teaspoon chopped parsley leaves

1 teaspoon garlic powder

¾ cup orzo

Pie Crust Dough

{ M A K E S 2 C R U S T S }

This recipe is our go-to pie crust dough for most of our pies. It makes
enough for one apple pie or chicken pot pie (which have two layers of crust)
or two other pies. For a vegan option, substitute a plant-based buttery
spread such as Earth Balance for the butter. The dough can last for up to
three days in the fridge or can be frozen for up to six months.

2½ cups all-purpose
flour

2 tablespoons
granulated sugar

1 teaspoon salt

16 tablespoons (2 sticks)
unsalted butter, cut into
1-inch pieces and chilled

¾ cup ice-cold water

Add the flour, sugar, and salt to a food processor.* Gently
pulse to combine. Add the chilled butter and pulse three
times. Very gradually add the ice-cold water to the crust
mix while pulsing. Continue to pulse until you have
added all of the water. Do not overblend. You should still
see small pieces of butter the size of peas when finished,
and the dough should be crumbly. (It is important to not
add all the water at once or the dough will become very
wet.) Wrap the dough tightly in plastic wrap and chill in
the fridge for 20 minutes or until ready to use.

*If you don't have a food processor, this recipe can
also be made by hand. Whisk together the flour, sugar, and
salt. Add the butter and cut with a pastry cutter or two knives
into pea-sized pieces. Slowly add the water, stirring all the
while, until the dough just comes together in your hand.*

Quiche

Since Kerber's Farm was originally a poultry farm producing lots and lots of eggs, homemade quiche has always been a popular menu item. This is an easy-to-prepare recipe that makes a nice lunch if served with a cup of soup or small salad.

Preheat the oven to 350°F.

Cut the pie dough in half. Wrap half and save it for later use. On a lightly floured surface, take the pie dough and roll it into a 10-inch circle. Carefully lift the dough and place it into a 9-inch pie plate. Tuck any excess crust underneath the edges and crimp with your fingers or a fork if desired.

In a saucepan set over medium-high heat, warm the olive oil. Then add the onions, ham, and mushrooms. Cook for approximately 5 minutes while stirring constantly until the onions are translucent and the mushrooms are cooked. Set aside to cool.

In a medium bowl, whisk the eggs and heavy cream together. Add the salt, sugar, and cayenne pepper and mix well. Put the onions, ham, mushrooms, and ½ cup cheddar cheese on the crust in the pan, spreading evenly. Pour the egg and cream mixture into the crust and mix slightly using a spoon. Top with the remaining cheddar ¼ cup cheese.

Bake for 40 to 45 minutes until the middle is slightly jiggly and a toothpick inserted in the center comes out clean. Allow to cool for a few minutes and then serve. It can be enjoyed hot, cold, or at room temperature.

1 pie crust dough
(see page 52)

2 tablespoons olive oil

¼ cup chopped onions

½ cup chopped ham

3 cups sliced mushrooms

2 eggs

1 cup heavy cream

½ teaspoon salt

¼ teaspoon granulated sugar

Pinch of ground cayenne pepper

½ cup shredded cheddar cheese, plus ¼ cup for topping

Overnight Oats

{ SERVES I }

This is a great breakfast or snack option that can be made ahead of time and grabbed as you head out in the morning. You can substitute the almond milk for any dairy or nut milk of your choice and customize the toppings.

1 cup oats

1 cup almond milk

¼ cup chopped almonds

¼ teaspoon ground cinnamon

2 tablespoons honey

½ cup fresh blueberries

In a sealable container such as a canning jar, add the oats, almond milk, almonds, and cinnamon. Mix well. Next, drizzle honey over the mixture, and then top with the blueberries. Do not mix. Place the lid on the jar and let it sit overnight or for at least six hours in the fridge. It can be stored up to two days.

SEEDLINGS

Growing plants at home and starting from just seeds can be a very rewarding and economical practice. Early each spring at Kerber's Farm, we purchase a variety of seeds and plant them in biodegradable trays indoors. We fill each hole of the tray with potting soil, leaving about ¼ inch of space at the top. Typically, we place two or three seeds in each hole, pushing them down slightly below the surface. Some larger plants only require one seed, such as cucumber, pumpkin, and melon. The trays are kept in a warm area, such as near a window with sunlight or under a heat lamp. Depending on the type of plant, the seeds typically germinate in 10 to 14 days and we soon see sprouting above the soil surface. When the seedlings have several true leaves on them, they can be transplanted outside in the garden. Most vegetable plants are ready for harvest in 90 to 100 days, while tomatoes are much faster at 60 to 70 days. The illustrations below show the stages of seedling growth.

Spinach Pie

{ SERVES 4 TO 6 }

My mother used to make this recipe for my family when I was growing up, and being of Greek descent, it is something I have always loved. The flakiness and crispness of the phyllo dough complements the warm and melted cheeses within. The taste of fresh dill is what makes it really special.

Preheat the oven to 375°F.

Heat a pan on medium-high heat and add the oil. Sauté the scallions for 5 minutes until fully cooked. Set aside to cool.

In a medium bowl, add the spinach, cheeses, eggs, dill, lemon juice, spices, and flour. Mix to combine well. Add the cooled scallions and mix again.

Brush the bottom of a 9-by-13-inch baking pan with some of the melted butter. Lay one sheet of phyllo dough in the bottom, and brush the top with butter. Add another sheet of phyllo, leaving some hanging over the sides of the pan, and brush with more butter. Repeat until only half of the phyllo dough remains.

Add the spinach mixture to the pan, spreading evenly, and then lift the overhanging edges of the phyllo dough so it can partially cover the mixture. Continue to add phyllo sheets, brushing with butter, until all sheets have been used. Once finished, brush the top with butter and place the pan in the oven.

Bake for approximately 45 minutes until golden brown. Let cool to room temperature and then cut to serve.

1 teaspoon olive oil

1 cup chopped scallions

3 (16-ounce) bags frozen spinach, defrosted and strained to remove excess water

2½ cups crumbled feta

1 cup cottage cheese

1¼ cups cream cheese, softened

5 eggs

2 tablespoons chopped fresh dill

2 teaspoons lemon juice

1 tablespoon salt

1 tablespoon pepper

1½ teaspoons garlic powder

1 tablespoon all-purpose flour

16 tablespoons (2 sticks) salted butter, melted

1 (16-ounce) package phyllo dough (14 by 18 inches), defrosted

Cheddar Buttermilk Biscuits

{ MAKES 12 BISCUITS }

A small café near my apartment in New York City always made a really great homemade biscuit. Each morning on my way to fix up the farm (before the store was reopened), I would purchase one and have it with my coffee. I wanted to make my own version for Kerber's Farm. I added cheese to the recipe, as well as some cayenne pepper to give it just a slight kick. These biscuits have been wildly successful, and have even caught Oprah's attention.

2 cups all-purpose flour

2 cups cake flour

1 tablespoon baking powder

1 tablespoon baking soda

1½ teaspoons salt

1½ teaspoons granulated sugar

1½ teaspoons garlic powder

¾ teaspoon cayenne pepper

16 tablespoons (2 sticks) unsalted butter, diced and chilled

1¼ pounds shredded cheddar jack cheese, plus extra for topping

2 cups buttermilk

2 tablespoons dijon mustard

SPECIAL EQUIPMENT:

3½-inch biscuit cutter

Preheat the oven to 350°F. Line a baking sheet with parchment paper or grease lightly.

In a medium bowl, add the flours, baking powder, baking soda, salt, sugar, garlic powder, and cayenne pepper. Whisk to combine. Using a pastry cutter or your fingers, knead the diced butter into the flour mixture until the pieces are the size of peas. Mix in the shredded cheese.

In a small bowl, whisk together the buttermilk and mustard. Pour the buttermilk mixture into the flour mixture, and then gently fold until they are just combined.

Place the dough on a well-floured surface and knead a few times to ensure all the ingredients are well mixed. Using a rolling pin, roll the dough out to a ½-inch thickness. Dip the biscuit cutter into the flour and then cut out the biscuits, using only an up-and-down motion. Avoid twisting the cutter to get the biscuits out (this will prevent the biscuits from rising as high).

Place the biscuits on the prepared baking sheet. Sprinkle the reserved cheese on top of each biscuit. Bake for 20 to 25 minutes, until the edges are lightly golden and the biscuits lift easily from the baking sheet.

Cheddar Buttermilk Biscuit Egg Sandwich

{ S E R V E S 4 }

Kerber's Farm has always been known for its fresh eggs, so we thought it
would be fitting to create a really amazing egg sandwich for our morning customers.
We use our cheddar biscuit as the base, and then add two perfectly fried
farm fresh eggs, bacon, American cheese, and sliced avocado.

Heat a large sauté pan over medium heat and add the oil.
Crack the eggs directly into the hot pan. Once the eggs are
cooked to your liking, add a slice of cheese to each egg.

Slice the biscuits. Place the eggs on the bottom of each
biscuit and then lay two pieces of bacon on top of the egg.

Cut the avocado into quarters (with the skin still on) and
slice each quarter. Lay one quarter of the avocado slices on
top of the bacon. Season with salt and pepper if desired.
Place the tops of the biscuits over the avocado and serve.

2 tablespoons olive oil

8 eggs

8 slices American cheese

4 cheddar buttermilk
biscuits (see page 62)

8 slices crispy bacon

2 ripe avocados, pitted

Salt and pepper
(optional)

Kerber's Cobb Salad

{ S E R V E S 4 }

This tasty play on the traditional Cobb salad is a derivation of a salad
I once served at a small café I owned in Oyster Bay, New York. The subtle notes of
pressed garlic and the tanginess of the dressing make this salad stand out.

FOR THE DRESSING:

1 cup mayonnaise

½ cup olive oil

¼ cup Grey Poupon mustard

¼ cup red wine vinegar

1 garlic clove, pressed

FOR THE SALAD:

1 (5-ounce) container arugula

1 pint grape tomatoes, halved

¼ cup chopped onion

½ cup crumbled Roquefort cheese

8 strips well-done bacon, coarsely chopped

4 hard-boiled eggs, peeled and cut into wedges

2 avocados, pitted, peeled, and cut into slices

Grilled chicken breast, sliced (optional)

To make the dressing, add all the ingredients to a bowl and mix thoroughly with a wire whisk.

To make the salad, toss the arugula with approximately ½ cup of the dressing in a large bowl. Divide the arugula among four chilled salad plates. For each salad, add equal amounts of the grape tomatoes, onion, cheese, and bacon. Top each salad with wedges from one egg and half an avocado. If desired, add slices of grilled chicken breast. Serve with additional dressing on the side.

FARMING

Kerber's Farm would not live up to its name if we did not continue its legacy of farming on this little plot of land on Long Island. The first chicken coop was built on the property in 1941, and we still raise chickens, ducks, and honeybees today. Kerber's began its life as a poultry farm and later added vegetables, fruit trees, and a pie shop. Although the farm no longer slaughters chickens for meat, we continue many of the original farming operations and raise numerous breeds of laying hens for fresh eggs.

Each year we get a batch of baby chicks from our local Agway, which we raise under a heat lamp in our farm stand. Once they are old enough to be outside, they are allowed to roam the property and nest in any one of the several barns we have. The older chickens stop laying eggs after several years and are allowed to live the rest of their lives in our sanctuary coop.

When we were restoring Kerber's Farm, we discovered the remnants of an old concrete pond shell under several feet of leaves and brush. We decided to clean the area out and restore the pond. We knew it would be the perfect place to keep ducks. The ducks we raise are Cayuga, and part of our current family was rescued from a farm in upstate New York. They are quite content in their new duck house and pond, and they often roam the property throughout the day.

Kerber's also maintains an organic garden that is partitioned into four equal quadrants, each separated by walking paths. In the quadrants we grow vegetables, herbs, wildflowers, and sunflowers. We have also begun to replace the numerous fruit trees and bushes—including apple, peach, and blueberry—that once existed on the property.

Early each spring we begin growing the plants for the garden indoors, where it is warmer. Under growing lights, we plant a variety of seeds in biodegradable potting trays that will germinate into small seedlings. Once it is warm enough outside and the seedlings have grown, the potting tray squares can be planted directly in the garden. We leave enough space between the rows for our power tiller to get by and turn over the inevitable weeds that grow. We also make a homemade organic weed killer with vinegar, orange oil, and soap. This is moderately effective when used with tilling, but some hand weeding is always needed close to the plants.

Kerber's Farm continues to thrive, and we hope to teach these practices to schoolchildren by building a farm education school on the property. The school will teach students the importance of sustainability, organic farming, and healthy eating habits.

Shepherd's Pie

This is our variation on a classic shepherd's pie, except we use ground beef instead of lamb. We find it has a less gamey flavor, and the more neutral ground beef brings all of the other ingredients together nicely. The subtle notes of Worcestershire and fresh rosemary allow this dish to truly stand out.

FOR THE TOPPING:

1½ pounds Yukon Gold potatoes, peeled and chopped

½ cup heavy cream, at room temperature

4 tablespoons (½ stick) salted butter, at room temperature

½ teaspoon pepper

1 egg yolk

2 teaspoons paprika

FOR THE FILLING:

2 tablespoons oil

1 cup chopped onion

1½ pounds ground beef

2 tablespoons all-purpose flour

1 teaspoon garlic powder

1 teaspoon pepper

1 teaspoon salt

1 teaspoon Frank's hot sauce

1 tablespoon granulated sugar

1 cup chicken stock

2 teaspoons finely chopped fresh rosemary

2 teaspoons

To make the topping, place the potatoes in a medium saucepan and cover with water. Place over medium heat and bring to a boil. Once the potatoes are boiling, reduce the heat and simmer until the potatoes are fork-tender. Drain the potatoes and place in a medium bowl. Mash the potatoes with a masher until smooth, and then add the cream, butter, pepper, and egg yolk. Mix until just combined and set aside.

Make the filling while the potatoes are boiling. Place a sauté pan over medium heat. Place the oil in the pan and add the onions. Cook approximately 5 minutes or until the onions are translucent and just browned. Add the ground beef and cook until browned. Add the flour. Mix well and cook for approximately 1 minute. Add the garlic powder, pepper, salt, hot sauce, sugar, chicken stock, rosemary, Worcestershire sauce, and tomato paste. Stir to combine. Add the peas and carrots. Mix well to heat the vegetables thoroughly. Let the mixture cool slightly.

Preheat the oven to 350°F.

Cut the pie dough in half. Wrap half and save for later use. On a lightly floured surface, take the dough and roll it into a 10-inch circle. Carefully lift the dough and place it in a 9-inch pie plate. Tuck any excess crust

underneath the edges and then crimp with your fingers or a fork if desired.

Add the cooled beef mixture evenly into the pie plate. Cover the filling with the mashed potatoes and then sprinkle paprika over the top. Place in the oven for 20 to 25 minutes. Garnish with parsley leaves.

Worcestershire sauce

1 tablespoon tomato paste

1 (12-ounce) frozen pea and carrot mix

1 pie crust dough (see page 52)

Parsley leaves, for garnish

Risotto with Asparagus and Mushrooms

{ SERVES 4 }

This hearty recipe is a one-dish meal perfect for when it is chilly outside.
The cream and chicken stock work in harmony to accentuate the wonderful flavors
of the mushrooms and asparagus. Serve with a salad if desired.

In a large, deep frying pan or saucepan, bring 2 cups of the chicken stock to a simmer over medium heat. Meanwhile, create an ice-water bath and set aside.

Add the asparagus and cook for 3 to 5 minutes, until it is bright green and slightly tender. Quickly remove the asparagus from the stock and place it in the ice-water bath to stop the cooking process. Once cool, cut into 1-inch pieces and discard the ends.

Transfer the chicken stock to a measuring cup and reserve. Set the pan on medium heat, melt the butter, and cook the onions until they are transparent. Add the rice to the pan, stirring and mixing until the onions and rice are slightly browned. Next, stir in the mushrooms and cook until they are tender.

Add the reserved stock to the rice and cover, stirring every few minutes. Once the stock is absorbed, add the remaining 4 cups stock and switch to low heat, stirring occasionally. When all of the stock has been absorbed and the rice is tender, add the cheese, cream, parsley, sugar, and pepper. Gently mix in the asparagus, taking care not to damage the delicate tips.

6 cups chicken stock

1 pound asparagus

2 tablespoons (¼ stick) salted butter

1 cup chopped onion

2 cups Arborio rice

3 cups sliced mushrooms (preferably shiitake)

¼ cup grated parmesan cheese

½ cup heavy cream

2 tablespoons chopped parsley leaves

¼ teaspoon granulated sugar

1 teaspoon pepper

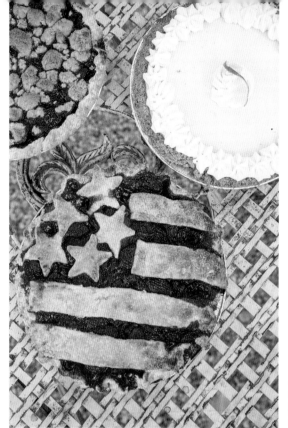

THE SUMMER SEASON AT KERBER'S FARM IS ONE OF THE MOST vibrant, where the fruits of our labor during the previous months can be seen literally every-where you look. A walk around the property highlights the essence of the season and all of the activities that go along with it.

Hydrangeas, snapdragons, sunflowers, and organic vegetables thrive in the gardens with the abundance of sunlight and warmth. The vegetable and herb seedlings that we planted during the spring show a glimpse of the wonderful harvest to come. The eggplant and zuc-chini plants have small flowers, and green tomatoes sprout almost daily. Aside from constant watering, most of the vegetable plants are self-sufficient except for the tomato plants, which must be tied and staked as they grow taller. The Kerber's Farm garden is organic and does not use fertilizer or any pesticides, so routine weeding is a laborious task.

By early June our honeybees are quite active, and one can witness a flurry of activity during the day. The bees quickly depart and return to their hives with the pollen they have gathered from nearby flowers. Inside the hive, a massive construction project is underway, with an army of worker bees building the vast network of honeycomb that will be used to store honey and lay eggs. By the end of July, enough honey has been made to have a harvest. This process usually takes two people and involves the bees being "smoked," which helps calm them so the hive can be accessed. The racks of honey are removed and brought into the barn, and a hot knife is used to remove the layer of wax that contains the honey. The racks are then spun in a centrifuge-type machine to collect the wonderful bounty. Last, the honey is jarred and put on the shelves in the store.

Over in the chicken coop, our baby chicks are now around six months old and beginning to lay their first eggs. Each chicken lays one egg per day. Hens are really easy to care for, only requiring a comfortable place to perch, good food, and fresh water. We give our hens an organic feed that we source from the local Agway store. Each morning, a staff member opens up the coop to let the chickens roam freely and then collects the eggs from the laying boxes. At night, the chickens are put back in the coop to protect them from raccoons, coyotes, and other predators.

Our store introduces summertime favorites beginning each Memorial Day and offers them through Columbus Day. Our tart and refreshing key lime pie is always a crowd-pleaser, as is our famous Kerberry Pie, which is made with three different types of berries. Since Kerber's Farm has always reminded me of places I've visited in Montauk, New York, or Nantucket, Massachusetts—usually by boat—I thought it would only be fitting to sell lobster rolls each summer. Each day, we receive a delivery of fresh Maine lobsters, which we use to make what has become one of our most popular items.

Visitors to Kerber's Farm are able to enjoy the warm weather and outdoor seating, tour the wonderful gardens, and interact with the chickens and ducks. Sitting outside among nature is a reminder of how special this part of the world is during the ever-fleeting summer.

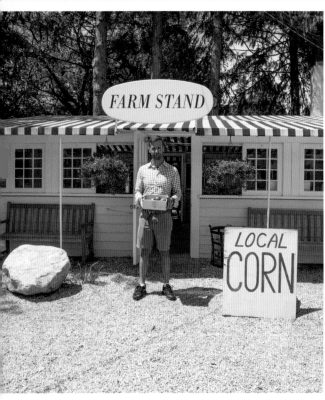

SUMMER RECIPES

Fresh-Squeezed Lemonade

{ MAKES 2 QUARTS }

Nothing says summer like a pitcher of fresh-squeezed lemonade—
although we serve this uberpopular drink all year long. Making lemonade at
home is an easy, more wholesome alternative to store-bought mixes.

1 cup granulated sugar

6 cups ice-cold water

1 cup fresh-squeezed
lemon juice (from 5 or
6 lemons)

Lemon slices, for garnish

Fresh mint, for garnish

Bring 1 cup of water to a boil in a small saucepan.
Immediately add the sugar and mix until dissolved.

Fill a pitcher with ice-cold water, and then add in the
sugar mixture and lemon juice. Stir to combine. Garnish
with lemon slices and fresh mint if desired.

Blueberry-Mint Ice Pops

{ MAKES TEN 2¼-OUNCE ICE POPS }

This is an easy summertime treat that everyone can enjoy, and it's fun for kids to help make. The simple three-ingredient recipe highlights some of the best flavors of the season. Purchase the ice-pop molds ahead of time so you have them on hand.

Add all the ingredients to a food processor or blender and pulse until the blueberries and mint are finely chopped. Carefully pour the mixture into the ice-pop molds and freeze them overnight.

To remove the pops from the molds, set them in warm water for 1 to 2 minutes, and then gently pull on the popsicle sticks to separate the pops from the molds.

2 cups fresh-squeezed lemonade (see page 86)

2 cups fresh blueberries

15 fresh mint leaves

SPECIAL EQUIPMENT:

10-pack ice-pop mold

10 popsicle sticks

Key Lime Pie

{ MAKES ONE 9-INCH PIE }

A summer favorite at Kerber's Farm, our key lime pie has a rich,
custard-like filling with flecks of lime zest. The sweet and tart key lime juice
is sure to delight your taste buds.

FOR THE CRUST:

1 cup graham cracker crumbs

¼ cup light brown sugar

5 tablespoons unsalted butter, melted

FOR THE FILLING:

8 ounces cream cheese, at room temperature

½ cup key lime juice

1 (15-ounce) can sweetened condensed milk

3 egg yolks

Zest of 1 lime

FOR THE TOPPING:

1 cup whipped cream (see page 133)

1 lime slice, for garnish

Preheat the oven to 350°F.

To make the crust, mix together the graham cracker crumbs and the brown sugar in a small bowl. Add the melted butter and stir together until combined. Add the crust mix to a 9-inch pie plate and press firmly around the plate. The crust should be approximately ¼-inch thick all the way around. Bake the crust for 5 minutes and then remove from the oven.

To make the filling, place the cream cheese in a stand mixer fitted with a paddle attachment and mix on medium speed. Slowly pour the lime juice into the cream cheese with the mixer running, stopping every minute or so to scrape the bowl with a spatula to prevent clumps. While continuing to mix, add the sweetened condensed milk, egg yolks, and zest. Mix until thoroughly combined.

Pour the filling into the crust and bake for 20 to 25 minutes, until lightly golden on top and the middle of the pie has only a slight jiggle. Let the pie cool to room temperature.

Add the whipped cream to a piping bag. Pipe the whipped cream around the edges and add one swirl in the middle. Using a knife, cut a slit in the lime slice. Twist the lime and place it in the center of the pie. Serve immediately.

Kerberry Pie

A play on our farm's namesake, this pie has become one of our most popular desserts, particularly after being featured in *O, The Oprah Magazine*. It is made with blueberries, raspberries, and strawberries. The sweet and tart flavors balance one another, and vanilla extract and cloves give this pie a wonderful down-home taste.

Preheat the oven to 350°F.

To make the topping, add the flour, sugars, cinnamon, and salt to a stand mixer fitted with a paddle attachment. With the mixer running on medium speed, add the cold butter and mix 6 to 7 minutes, until large clumps form. Transfer to a bowl and cover in the fridge until ready to use.

Cut the pie dough in half. Wrap one half and save for later use. On a lightly floured surface, roll out the dough into a 10-inch circle. Carefully lift the dough, place it in a 9-inch pie plate, and form to the plate. Tuck any excess crust underneath the edges and crimp with your fingers or a fork.

To make the filling, add the berries to a medium bowl and gently mix. Add the sugar, vanilla, spices, zest, and tapioca starch and mix to combine. Pour the filling into the pie crust and spread evenly with a spatula. Next, add the crumb topping in an even layer.

Bake the pie for approximately 30 minutes, and then take it out and cover it with foil. Bake it for an additional 45 minutes, and then let it cool to room temperature.

FOR THE TOPPING:

1 cup all-purpose flour

¼ cup granulated sugar

½ cup light brown sugar

½ teaspoon ground cinnamon

¼ teaspoon salt

8 tablespoons (1 stick) cold unsalted butter, diced

1 pie crust dough (see page 52)

FOR THE FILLING:

¾ pound blueberries

¾ pound raspberries

¾ pound strawberries

½ cup granulated sugar

1½ teaspoons vanilla extract

½ teaspoon ground cloves

½ teaspoon ground cinnamon

1 teaspoon orange zest

2 tablespoons tapioca starch

Kerberry Jam

{ MAKES APPROXIMATELY TEN 8-OUNCE JARS }

This recipe is for our Kerberry Jam. The idea came from my good friend
Rob Levy, who was helping me paint the store during the summer of 2013. He simply
said, "You should have a jam called Kerberry!" and its fate was sealed.
It took two and a half years to refine the recipe and finally launch the product,
and then the jam made Oprah's coveted "Favorite Things" list in March 2016.

2 pounds blueberries

2 pounds raspberries

2 pounds strawberries

1 cup granulated sugar

½ cup light brown sugar

½ teaspoon ground
cloves

½ teaspoon ground
cinnamon

⅓ cup pectin

1 teaspoon orange zest

1 teaspoon lemon juice

1 teaspoon vanilla
extract

SPECIAL EQUIPMENT:

10 (8-ounce) canning
jars and lids

Candy thermometer

In a large saucepan, bring 1 gallon of water to a boil.
Once the water is boiling, carefully place the jars and lids
in the pan and continue to boil for 5 minutes to sterilize.
After 5 minutes, carefully remove the jars from the water
and place them upside down on a drying rack.

Wash all the fruit, and cut the strawberries into quarters.
Place the fruit in a saucepan over medium-high heat and
stir frequently. Attach a candy thermometer to the pan.

In a separate bowl, mix the sugars, spices, and
pectin together.

Let the fruit cook for approximately 15 minutes until it
comes to a rolling boil that cannot be stirred down. Add
the dry ingredients, stirring all the while. Let the jam
boil for 1 minute. Once it boils, mix in the zest, lemon
juice, and vanilla. Bring the jam up to 180°F. Once it has
reached temperature, remove it from the heat.

Using a pitcher, carefully scoop the jam out of the
saucepan, pour it into the jars, and cap them. Place
the jars back in boiling water for approximately
10 minutes to complete the canning process. (For more
information about canning, see page 134.)

The Kerber's Farm Cookbook • 94

Cold Gazpacho Soup

{ S E R V E S 4 }

This is an all-time summer favorite that I have been making for more than
20 years. It's a refreshing option to have on a hot summer day,
and the wonderful flavors of the cilantro, tomato, and seeds from the
garden peppers will have you smacking your lips for more! To make this soup
vegan or vegetarian, substitute vegetable stock for the beef stock.

In a large bowl, whisk together the tomato purée and
beef stock.

In a food processor, add the carrot, squash, peppers
(with seeds), and onion and pulse until finely chopped.
Add the chopped vegetable mixture to the bowl and
whisk together. Mix in ½ cup chopped cilantro and the
remaining ingredients, adjusting the Tabasco sauce to
your desired level of heat. Garnish with the remaining
2 tablespoons chopped cilantro.

2 (28-ounce) cans
tomato purée, chilled

2 cups beef stock, chilled

1 large carrot, peeled
and cut into 1-inch
pieces

1 large green squash,
cut into 1-inch pieces

1 red pepper, cut
into 1-inch slices
(reserve the seeds)

1 yellow pepper, cut
into 1-inch slices
(reserve the seeds)

½ cup chopped white
onion

½ cup chopped cilantro,
plus 2 tablespoons for
garnish

1 tablespoon salt

½ teaspoon pepper

½ teaspoon granulated
sugar

2 teaspoons Tabasco
sauce (or to taste)

Clams on the Half Shell

{ S E R V E S 4 T O 6 }

One of the joys of life near the sea is being able to catch and eat fresh clams. Clamming was always one of my favorite parts of summer when I was growing up. My father would take my brother and I out in our dinghy and head for the muddy shallows near the salt marsh. We would dig for clams in waist-high water with a rake, or simply use our feet to feel for them. The experience of digging for clams was just as great as the treat of eating them later. Paul Kerber also used to send his two sons out to Eatons Neck on Long Island's North Shore to dig for clams so they could use them in the store. This simple recipe includes my favorite easy-to-make cocktail sauce.

1 cup Heinz ketchup

3 tablespoons lemon juice

2 tablespoons jarred horseradish

½ teaspoon Worcestershire sauce

½ teaspoon Tabasco sauce

1 teaspoon coarsely ground black pepper

2 dozen littleneck clams, chilled and shucked

Lemon wedges, for garnish

Mix the ketchup, lemon juice, horseradish, Worcestershire sauce, Tabasco sauce, and pepper thoroughly in a small bowl. Arrange the clams on a chilled plate or on a bed of crushed ice. Place a small dollop of cocktail sauce on each clam. Garnish with lemon wedges.

TYPES OF
C L A M S

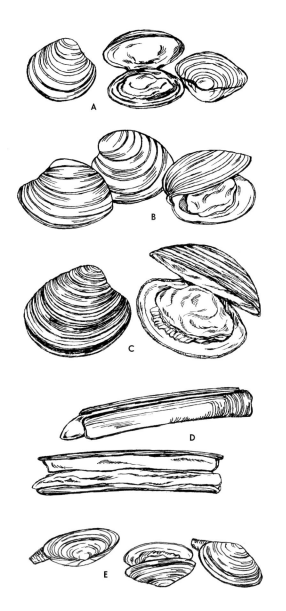

These wonderful and tasty treasures of the sea live mostly buried below the water's surface on the seabed or in tidal flats in sand or mud. Digging them up can be a fun activity in the summer months.

A. LITTLE NECK: These are the smallest of the clam family. They are often considered the tastiest, which is why they are shucked and eaten raw for clams on the half shell.

B. CHERRY STONE: These medium-sized clams are great for using in sauces or steamed or grilled open.

C. QUAHOG: These very large clams can measure up to four or five inches wide and are often chopped up and used in chowders.

D. RAZOR: Often overlooked, these elongated clams get their name from their resemblance to vintage razors. Their meat is tasty and can be used in a variety of dishes.

E. STEAMER: Also known as Ipswich clams, these whitish, soft-shell clams are identifiable by their external "neck." Like the name suggests, these clams are often steamed open and then dipped in melted butter.

Endive and Citrus Salad

{ SERVES 4 }

I love this simple, refreshing summer salad. The anise flavor of the
fennel is softened nicely by the sweetness of the orange juice in the dressing.
Depending on your flavor preference, you can choose to add
orange or grapefruit wedges as a garnish.

FOR THE SALAD:

2 heads fennel, cut into
¼-inch slices

4 heads endive, cut into
1-inch pieces

1 orange or grapefruit,
peeled and cut into
½-inch wedges, for
garnish

FOR THE DRESSING:

⅓ cup fresh-squeezed
orange juice (from
1 orange)

⅓ cup olive oil

½ teaspoon salt

½ teaspoon pepper

1 teaspoon parsley
leaves

To make the salad, toss the fennel and endive in a
medium bowl and set aside.

To make the dressing, combine all the ingredients
and mix in a small bowl with a whisk.

Add half of the dressing to the fennel and endive
and toss. Plate the salad and garnish with the
orange or grapefruit wedges. Serve with additional
dressing on the side.

Dill Potato Salad

{ S E R V E S   4   T O   6 }

I grew up working in a deli after school, and dill potato salad was one
of the biggest sellers. I like using red potatoes, as I find them to be sweeter
and less dry than other varieties. This recipe makes a great side dish
to serve at summer barbecues and picnics.

In a large saucepan, bring 3 quarts of water to a boil.
Reduce the heat to medium and add the potatoes.
Cook until the potatoes are fork-tender, approximately
40 minutes. Drain and then cool the potatoes under
cold water.

Do not peel the skin, but cut the potatoes into
bite-sized cubes approximately ¾ inch thick and place
them in a bowl. Add the remaining ingredients and
gently mix, taking care not to smash the potatoes.

3 pounds red potatoes

1½ cups mayonnaise

½ cup chopped dill

1 tablespoon white
vinegar

1 teaspoon salt

1 teaspoon granulated
sugar

1 teaspoon pepper

Corn and Mango Salad

{ SERVES 4 TO 6 }

This is one of my favorite summer salads, and it is so simple to make.
I choose not to cook the corn, which allows its true flavor to
shine through. I happen to love cilantro, but I know it's not for everyone,
so you can substitute fresh mint or parsley if desired.

8 ears corn

1 red pepper, diced into
¼-inch pieces

2 fresh mangoes, peeled
and diced into ½-inch
cubes

¼ cup chopped cilantro

¼ cup vegetable oil

2 tablespoons chopped
red onion

1½ teaspoons salt

1½ teaspoons pepper

Remove the husks from the corn. With a sharp knife,
slice off all the kernels and place them in a bowl. Add the
remaining ingredients and mix well. Serve chilled or at
room temperature.

HONEYBEES

I knew when I purchased Kerber's Farm that I wanted to have honeybees on the property. The idea of becoming a beekeeper and producing honey appealed to me, and those wonderful painted wooden hives would be pretty additions to the gardens.

Around the same time that I bought Kerber's, the honeybee was on the cover of *Time*, warning of the perils these vital insects were facing. Hives were dying around the world, which had scientists extremely concerned. It's not entirely clear what is causing this problem, but evidence points to climate change, Varroa mites, disease, or overuse of pesticides.

Bees pollinate approximately 70 percent of the crops that are the food source for 90 percent of the world. If bees were to vanish, the crops that humans and livestock consume would also vanish. This epidemic would quickly move up the food chain, and humans would starve. Reading about this was alarming, and it reinforced my desire to raise bees.

During the six months of construction to get the store reopened, strangers and friends would stop by, curious about what I was doing with the old place. As part of the tour I was happy to give, I would tell everyone about my desire to restore the organic vegetable garden, have chickens and ducks, and, of course, raise honeybees.

As luck would have it, a friend of a friend was a local beekeeper and she was moving out of state. She had several beehives that she could not take with her and was looking for a good home for them. We were introduced, and she agreed to give me the bees after some hands-on instruction on caring for them and their hives.

I visited her home, donned a bee suit, and over the course of several visits learned all I could about honeybees and harvesting honey. Then at dusk one evening, when the bees were quiet, we wrapped each hive in canvas, carefully loaded them into the back of my pickup truck, and transported them to a field at Kerber's Farm.

Having bees and caring for them is immensely rewarding. Being witness to the construction of the beautiful and perfectly symmetrical honeycomb that they build is a miracle and a testament to Mother Nature. After tasting honey that comes out of a local hive, you will never want to buy commercial honey again. For the most part, honeybees are quite self-sufficient; with just a little care, they can be a great addition to your backyard, garden, or urban rooftop.

Country Coleslaw

{ S E R V E S 4 T O 6 }

A staple at any summer picnic, this recipe is great as a side dish or incorporated into sandwiches to add both a crunchy texture and a dressing. The shredded cabbage can release a lot of water over time, so I recommend making this dish no more than an hour in advance or it may need to be drained.

Place the shredded cabbage, carrot, and parsley in a large bowl. In a separate medium bowl, add the remaining ingredients. Mix well with a whisk, and then combine with the vegetables. Mix well again.

1 head cabbage, shredded

1 cup shredded carrot

½ cup chopped parsley leaves

½ cup mayonnaise

2 tablespoons vegetable oil

3 tablespoons white vinegar

1 tablespoon salt

1 tablespoon pepper

1½ teaspoons granulated sugar

Lobster Rolls

{ SERVES 4 }

I spent a lot of summer days on boats with my family when I was growing up.
We would visit places like Montauk, New York; Block Island, Rhode Island;
and Nantucket, Massachusetts—where small rambling shacks would serve lobster rolls.
I wanted to incorporate those memories and my love of the sea at Kerber's Farm,
so I added this iconic dish to our menu. It was written up in *The New York Times* and
voted one of the best lobster rolls on Long Island. Our secret is using the freshest
Maine lobster and Martin's potato rolls. The rolls are lightly buttered and grilled, which
browns the surface and caramelizes the natural sugars in the bread.

2 (1½-pound) Maine lobsters

¼ cup mayonnaise

1 tablespoon lemon juice

3 tablespoons finely chopped celery

Pinch of salt (or to taste)

½ teaspoon pepper

¼ teaspoon granulated sugar

2 tablespoons (¼ stick) salted butter, softened

4 Martin's hot dog potato rolls

2 cups shredded iceberg lettuce

In a large pot on high heat, bring 8 quarts of water to a rolling boil. Place the lobsters in the water and allow them to cook for several minutes. When they float to the top, they are ready. Using tongs, remove them from the pot and cool under cold water.

Remove all the meat from the tails, knuckles, and claws and chop into bite-sized pieces. (I like to keep the tips of the claw meat intact for visual appeal.) Transfer the meat to a bowl and mix in the mayonnaise, lemon juice, celery, salt, pepper, and sugar.

Lightly butter the inside of the potato rolls and place them facedown in a frying pan on medium heat. Cook for 2 to 3 minutes or until they brown, taking care not to burn them.

Line each roll with a bed of shredded lettuce and then add a healthy scoop of the lobster salad.

Roasted Salmon with Sour Cream Dill Sauce

{ SERVES 4 }

This tasty summer dish is easy to make and a great alternative to meats. The versatility of salmon makes it ideal for searing, baking, poaching, or grilling. This recipe is baked in the oven. The lemon juice and fresh dill add wonderful layers of flavor.

Preheat the oven to 450°F.

To make the salmon, place the fillets in a deep dish or bowl and gently mix with the oil, lemon juice, salt, and pepper until the fish is well coated. Place the fillets on a nonstick baking sheet and bake until cooked through, 12 to 15 minutes.

To make the sauce, whisk together the sour cream and heavy cream in a medium bowl. Add the salt, pepper, dill, and sugar and whisk thoroughly.

Serve each fillet with a dollop of the sour cream dill sauce and garnish with lemon slices and dill sprigs.

FOR THE SALMON:

4 skinless salmon fillets (approximately ½ pound each)

3 tablespoons vegetable oil

2 tablespoons lemon juice

¼ teaspoon salt

¼ teaspoon pepper

FOR THE SAUCE:

1 cup sour cream

1 tablespoon heavy cream

½ teaspoon salt

½ teaspoon pepper

1 tablespoon chopped fresh dill

Pinch of granulated sugar

Lemon slices, for garnish

Sprigs of dill, for garnish

Potato Chip–Crusted Fried Chicken

{ MAKES 10 PIECES }

This is a great dish to make ahead of time and pack for a family outing or picnic. The homemade coating has a great flavor and texture, and the chicken can be served at room temperature, warm, or chilled.

1 (5½-pound) chicken, cut into 10 pieces, with the backbone and wing tips removed

2 (8-ounce) bags kettle-cooked potato chips

2 tablespoons paprika

1 tablespoon granulated garlic

2 teaspoons pepper

2 teaspoons salt, plus more for finishing

1 teaspoon Cajun seasoning

¾ cup light brown sugar

1 cup all-purpose flour

1 teaspoon granulated sugar

3 eggs

8 cups canola oil, for frying

SPECIAL EQUIPMENT:

Candy thermometer

Instant-read thermometer

Thoroughly dry the pieces of chicken with paper towels.

Using a food processor or your hands, crush the potato chips and add to a medium bowl. To the crushed chips, add the paprika, garlic, 1 teaspoon of the pepper, 1 teaspoon of the salt, the Cajun seasoning, and brown sugar. Mix together. In another bowl, add the flour, the remaining 1 teaspoon pepper and salt, and the sugar. Whisk together. In a third bowl, add the eggs and 1 tablespoon of water. Blend together with a fork. Set the three bowls up in the following order: the seasoned flour first, the eggs second, and the chip mixture third.

In a cast-iron or heavy skillet fitted with a candy thermometer, add the oil and heat to 325°F. Working with one piece of chicken at a time, dip into the flour bowl first, shaking to remove any excess flour, and then into the egg bowl. Finally, coat the chicken generously with the potato chip mixture before placing on a baking sheet. Repeat the process until all pieces are thoroughly coated.

Working with four or five pieces at a time to avoid overcrowding the pan, gently lay the chicken in the hot oil. Be sure the oil remains around 325°F by adjusting the heat as needed. Keep turning the pieces every 1 to 2 minutes until they are deep golden brown and an instant-read thermometer registers 165°F. Breasts, legs, and thighs take

approximately 12 minutes to cook, and wings take about 10 minutes. Once the chicken is done, remove the pieces from the oil and place on a cooling rack or paper towels. Season immediately with a pinch of salt while still hot.

FALL

EXTRA VIRGIN OLIVE OIL
EXTRA VIRGIN OLIVE OIL
EXTRA VIRGIN OLIVE OIL
BALSAMIC VINEGAR
BALSAMIC VINEGAR

Extra Virgin
Olive Oil
$21.00

Balsamic
Vinegar

HOMEMADE PIES

Apple	Cherry Crumb
Strawberry Rhubarb	Korberry
Coconut Cream	Blueberry Crumb
S'Mores	Apple Crumb
Peach	Key Lime

GROUND FRESH

As Kerber's is a working farm with the nostalgia of an old-fashioned farm stand, the fall season is the busiest time of year for us. Long Island has lost many of its farms to development in the last few decades, but fortunately for us there has been a renewed interest in frequenting these community treasures. It seems the public now more than ever craves locally sourced food and a wholesome interactive experience that the whole family can appreciate.

As soon as Labor Day passes and the air becomes more brisk, we begin to offer all of the wonderful fall products found at a rural farm stand, plus some that are unique to Kerber's Farm. Outside, the sunflowers we have been growing all summer are harvested and then sold by the bunch in our shop. The fields are filled with pumpkins for people to pick, and we sell mums, cornstalks, and an assortment of apples and fall squashes. We set up hay bales for children to play on, and we offer other outdoor activities such as cornhole, horseshoe throwing, and potato-sack races.

To nourish everyone after these activities, our shop's café and bakery offers tasty fall treats such as hot apple cider, pumpkin pie, candied apples, and butternut squash soup.

We do quite a bit of canning this time of year and make many varieties of jam, including apple, cherry, fig, and strawberry rhubarb. We also do a final honey harvest in the fall, packaging hundreds of jars of honey to sell. We then "winterize" the bees by closing up their hives so they stay warm and hibernate, and we give them a food source such as sugar water to help them get through the long, cold winter.

After the final crop of vegetables has been harvested, we prepare our organic vegetable garden for the winter. All of the tomato stakes and sign markers are removed from the fields and safely stored in one of the barns. We use a power tiller to turn over all of the beds one final time and then plant rye seed. The rye helps control topsoil erosion and balances nitrogen levels. It also has an added benefit: our ducks and chickens love to forage on it when they are out roaming!

As the season moves closer to November, all focus turns to Thanksgiving pies. Our little shop prepares thousands of pies that are sold in the days leading up to the holiday. Each pie is individually handmade using the recipes found in this book. Classics such as apple and pumpkin are always popular, as are newer creations such as Kerberry and coconut cream. We also prepare many side dishes that incorporate mushrooms or root vegetables to accompany a traditional Thanksgiving dinner.

The fall season signals the end of warm weather and the shift to cooler, shorter days—and for some this can be a difficult transition. We hope these recipes help you embrace this change as you pull out those sweaters, enjoy the fall colors, and spend quality time at home.

FALL RECIPES

Apple Cider Doughnuts

Apple cider doughnuts have been a fall favorite of mine ever since I can remember. They are a staple at many farm stands around Long Island, and I think you will really love this version. At Kerber's, we add our apple pie filling into the dough before frying.

FOR THE DOUGH:

3½ cups all-purpose flour

2½ teaspoons baking powder

¾ teaspoon baking soda

½ teaspoon salt

1½ teaspoons pumpkin spice

3 cups chopped apple slices or apple pie filling (see page 136)

2 eggs

½ cup light brown sugar

¾ cup apple cider

3 tablespoons unsalted butter, melted

6 cups vegetable oil, for cooking

FOR THE TOPPING:

½ cup granulated sugar

½ cup light brown sugar

1½ teaspoons pumpkin spice

1 cup apple cider

SPECIAL EQUIPMENT:

Candy thermometer

3.5-inch cutter

1-inch cutter

To make the dough, whisk together the flour, baking powder, baking soda, salt, and pumpkin spice in a medium bowl. Next, add the chopped apples or apple pie filling and gently mix. Set aside.

In a small bowl, whisk together the eggs and sugar, and then add the apple cider and butter. Add the wet mixture to the flour mixture and mix thoroughly to form the dough.

In a medium saucepan, add the oil and heat on medium high until 325°F, checking the temperature with a candy thermometer. While oil is heating, begin to roll out the doughnuts.

On a well-floured surface, roll out the dough to ½-inch thickness. Cut out the doughnuts with the large cutter, and then cut out the centers with the smaller cutter. Place the doughnuts on a lightly floured baking sheet.

To make the topping, mix together the sugars and pumpkin spice in a small bowl. Pour apple cider in another bowl. Set both aside for dipping.

Once oil is at temperature, gently place the doughnuts in the pan, taking care not to overcrowd it (three to four doughnuts at a time). Cook each side for 2 to 3 minutes. Place the doughnuts on a cooling rack or paper towels.

While the doughnuts are warm, dip each in apple cider, tapping gently over the bowl to remove any excess cider. Then coat with the spiced sugar mix.

Pumpkin Pie

Synonymous with harvest time and cooler temperatures, pumpkin pie
possesses the wonderful flavor profile we have become accustomed
to in the fall season. The Kerber's version has a rich shortbread crust and all
of the classic spices, including cinnamon, nutmeg, ginger, and cloves.

FOR THE CRUST:

8 tablespoons (1 stick)
unsalted butter, softened

¼ cup powdered sugar

1 cup all-purpose flour

FOR THE FILLING:

1 (15-ounce) can pumpkin

2 eggs

¾ cup granulated sugar

¼ cup light brown sugar

1 teaspoon salt

2 teaspoons ground
cinnamon

½ teaspoon ground
ginger

1 pinch ground nutmeg

1 pinch ground cloves

½ cup whole milk

¼ cup sweetened
condensed milk

FOR THE TOPPING:

2 cups whipped cream
(see opposite page)

Ground cinnamon,
for garnish

Preheat the oven to 350°F.

To make the shortbread crust, combine the butter and
sugar in a stand mixer fitted with a paddle attachment.
Mix on medium speed until fluffy. Reduce the mixer
speed to medium-low, add the flour, and mix until
all of the flour is combined.

On a lightly floured surface, roll the dough into a
10-inch circle. Gently lift the dough and place it in a
9-inch pie plate, trimming any excess dough hanging
over the edges. Prick the dough all over with a fork to
prevent excessive puffing. Place on a baking sheet and
bake for 20 minutes until lightly golden. While the
shortbread is baking, you can prepare the filling.

To make the filling, add the pumpkin and eggs to a
medium bowl and whisk together. Add the sugars, salt,
cinnamon, ginger, nutmeg, and cloves. Mix well. Add
the milks and mix well again.

Once the shortbread is baked, add the filling to
the hot crust and place it back in the oven. Bake for
40 to 45 minutes, until a knife inserted in the center
comes out clean.

Let the pie cool to room temperature. Use a piping
bag to decorate with whipped cream and, if desired,
garnish with a few sprinkles of ground cinnamon.

Whipped Cream

Makes 1 ½ to 2 cups

Place all of the ingredients in a stand mixer fitted with a whisk attachment. Mix on high speed for approximately 1 minute, until stiff peaks form. Take care not to overbeat; watch the mixer closely.

Use the whipped cream immediately or place in the fridge for later use. (Tip: Place the whisk and bowl in the freezer for 20 minutes before starting.)

1 cup cold heavy cream

2 tablespoons light brown sugar

½ teaspoon vanilla extract

CANNING

The practice of canning food dates back to the early 1800s in France, when Napoleon saw the need to effectively distribute rations to army soldiers. The French government offered a large reward to any inventor who could devise a method of effectively preserving food for this use. In 1809, French brewer and candymaker Nicolas Appert won the prize when he proved that food cooked in a glass jar would not spoil if properly sealed.

Canning and preserving was soon adopted in other parts of Europe and eventually in the United States. In 1812, a canning factory opened in New York City that implemented tin cans to preserve various cooked meats and vegetables.

The process of heating food in a sealed container while submerged in boiling water removes the ability of microorganisms to grow bacteria. As the jar cools, the remaining air inside contracts and forms a vacuum seal.

Canning can be used to preserve most food items. It is popular in home kitchens for garden vegetables, jams, and fruits. At Kerber's Farm, we frequently can surplus vegetables from our garden, as well as jams, sauces, and pie fillings. Here are the basic instructions we use to can our apple pie filling (see page 136) if you'd like to try it at home:

1. Submerge a 20-ounce jar and lid in boiling water for approximately 5 minutes to sanitize. Remove it from the water and allow it to dry.

2. Heat the apple pie filling to 180°F.

3. Fill the jar with the filling, leaving approximately ½ inch of space at the top. Wipe any drips off the jar edge with a clean rag and hand-tighten the lid.

4. Carefully place the sealed jar back into boiling water for approximately 10 minutes, ensuring that the jar is fully submerged.

5. Remove the jar and place it on a cooling rack. Within a few hours, you should hear a popping sound as the air contracts and the lid button depresses.

Apple Pie

Not surprisingly, apple pie is America's favorite, and it's also the most
popular pie at Kerber's Farm (although our Kerberry is usually a close second).
Kerber's Farm has been making apple pies since the 1940s, and this recipe
is pretty close to the original except that Evelyn Kerber's version called for
lard instead of butter. For a vegan option, skip the egg wash and substitute
a plant-based buttery spread such as Earth Balance for the butter.

1½ pounds tart apples, washed, peeled, cored, and sliced

¾ cup granulated sugar, plus more for dusting

1½ teaspoons ground cinnamon

½ teaspoon ground cloves

½ teaspoon ground nutmeg

2 teaspoons vanilla extract

¼ cup tapioca starch

1 egg, for wash

1 pie crust dough (see page 52)

In a small pot on medium to low heat, add the apples
and cook for 20 to 25 minutes, stirring frequently. Once
the apples are softened, add the sugar, spices, and vanilla
and stir. Remove from the heat and set aside.

In a bowl, combine the tapioca starch and ¼ cup
water to form a milky paste. Add to the apple mixture
and gently stir. Let the apple pie filling cool to room
temperature or place in the refrigerator until cool.

Preheat the oven to 350°F.

In a small bowl, mix together the egg and 1 tablespoon
water. Set aside.

Remove the pie dough from the refrigerator and cut it
into two equal halves. Lightly dust the countertop with
flour and roll out each piece of dough to a 10-inch circle
approximately ⅛ inch thick. Carefully lift one rolled-out
crust and place in a 9-inch pie plate. Gently shape to the
form of the plate. Pour the cooled apple pie filling onto
the crust. Place the second circle of dough over the top
of the pie, trimming any excess dough that hangs over.
Tuck and crimp the edges along the perimeter of the pie
crust. Cut an X or your desired shape into the middle

of the top crust to vent the pie while cooking. Brush with the egg wash and dust with granulated sugar.

Transfer the pie to a baking sheet and set in the oven. Bake for 25 to 30 minutes, and then cover the pie with foil and continue baking for an additional 45 minutes. Remove the pie from the oven and let cool to room temperature uncovered.

Candied Apples

{ MAKES 6 APPLES }

This easy fall snack may just make going back to school a little bit easier.
It is believed candied apples were invented by a candymaker in
Newark, New Jersey, and became popular along the New Jersey shore
in the early 1900s. They continue to be a popular snack, and their arrival
each year is an indicator of the fall season.

6 green apples

1 cup granulated sugar

½ cup light corn syrup

6 drops red food
coloring

2 teaspoons ground
cinnamon

SPECIAL EQUIPMENT:

6 popsicle sticks

Candy thermometer

Wash and dry the apples very well, as moisture will
prevent the sugar coating from sticking. Remove the
stems and insert popsicle sticks. Spray a small baking
sheet with baking spray.

In a medium pot over medium heat, combine the sugar,
corn syrup, and ¾ cup water.

Using a candy thermometer, bring the mixture to 300 to
310°F. (If you don't have a thermometer, you can test
by dropping a small amount of the syrup into cold water.
It should form brittle threads.) Once the syrup comes to
temperature, immediately remove the pot from the heat
and add red food coloring and cinnamon.

Working quickly but carefully, hold each apple by
the stick and dip into the syrup, turning to ensure
complete coverage. Place on the prepared baking sheet
to let harden.

Ginger Molasses Cookies

{ MAKES APPROXIMATELY 18 COOKIES }

This cookie is a Kerber's Farm favorite. Its moist and chewy consistency, coupled with the molasses and ginger notes, will quickly transport you back to a simpler time.

Preheat the oven to 350°F. Line a baking sheet with parchment paper.

In a small bowl, whisk together the flour, baking soda, spices, and salt. Set aside.

In a stand mixer fitted with a paddle attachment, add the butter and brown sugar. Mix on medium speed until light and fluffy. Scrape down the sides with a rubber spatula. Add the egg and molasses and mix until just combined, scraping down the sides with the spatula as needed. With the mixer running on low speed, slowly add the dry ingredients and continue to mix until just combined.

Portion out cookies and form into the size of a golf ball. Roll each in crystal sugar and place on the prepared baking sheet. Flatten each cookie slightly using your palms.

Bake for 15 to 17 minutes, until a toothpick inserted in the center comes out clean. Let cool to room temperature.

1½ cups all-purpose flour

2 teaspoons baking soda

1½ teaspoons ground ginger

1 teaspoon ground cinnamon

½ teaspoon salt

12 tablespoons (1½ sticks) unsalted butter, softened

½ cup light brown sugar

1 egg

¼ cup molasses

¼ cup crystal sugar, for rolling

Farm Carrot Muffins

If you love carrot cake, you will love this recipe for wholesome
carrot muffins with pecans, shredded coconut, and raisins. The use of
classic spices gives this muffin a nostalgic flavor, and it makes a
great breakfast item or after-school treat. For a vegan version, substitute
a mashed banana in place of the egg and use almond milk.

1 cup all-purpose flour

½ cup granulated sugar

3 tablespoons light brown sugar

2 teaspoons ground cinnamon

¼ teaspoon ground ginger

⅛ teaspoon baking soda

1½ teaspoons baking powder

⅛ teaspoon salt

¾ cup shredded carrots

¼ cup shredded coconut flakes

½ cup raisins

⅓ cup chopped pecans

½ cup vegetable oil

1 egg

¼ cup milk

2 teaspoons vanilla extract

Preheat the oven to 350°F.

In a stand mixer or small bowl, whisk together the flour, sugars, cinnamon, ginger, baking soda, baking powder, and salt. Next, add the carrots, coconut flakes, raisins, and chopped pecans. Mix to combine.

In another bowl or a liquid measuring cup, combine the vegetable oil, egg, milk, and vanilla. Whisk until blended. Add the wet ingredients to the dry ingredients and fold until just combined.

Spray a muffin pan with baking spray or line with baking liners. Fill each muffin cup one-third of the way full with batter.

Bake for 25 to 30 minutes, until a knife inserted in the center comes out clean. Let cool to room temperature before removing from the pan.

Butternut Squash Soup

{ MAKES 2 QUARTS }

This is an easy, no-nonsense version of a classic fall soup that can be
made very quickly in one pot. It is a top seller at Kerber's Farm and makes
a great lunch when paired with our dinner roll or cheddar biscuit.

In a medium pot, add the squash and vegetable stock.
Bring to a boil. Reduce the heat, cover the pot, and
let simmer until the pieces of squash are fork-tender,
35 to 40 minutes.

Remove from the heat. In small batches, transfer the
stock and squash to a blender and blend until smooth
(do not drain). If you have an immersion blender,
place it in the pot and blend until completely smooth
and no lumps remain.

Return the stock and squash mixture to the pot over low
heat. Add the salt, cinnamon, pepper, and cream and mix.
Cook for approximately 20 more minutes on low heat
to combine the flavors. If a sweeter flavor is desired, add
brown sugar. Add parsley leaves for garnish.

1 large butternut
squash (approximately
4 pounds), washed,
peeled, and chopped
into 1-inch pieces

6 cups vegetable stock
(or chicken stock if
desired)

1 teaspoon salt

2 teaspoons ground
cinnamon

1½ teaspoons pepper

½ cup heavy cream

1 tablespoon light brown
sugar (optional)

Parsley leaves, for
garnish

Roasted Brussels Sprouts

{ SERVES 4 }

I first had brussels sprouts when I was probably eight years old, and I must say I was not a fan. I remember they were boiled in water and tasted soggy and unappealing. I have since learned to love this vegetable as a great complement to any meal using this simple recipe. I prefer to cook them until they are just beyond well done, but not quite burnt. The natural sugars the sprouts contain caramelize on the outside, and the outer leaves become light and flaky. We offer this side dish at Kerber's Farm as part of our Thanksgiving menu, and we always run out!

3 (12-ounce) packages brussels sprouts

½ cup vegetable oil

⅓ cup grated parmesan cheese

1½ teaspoons salt

1½ teaspoons coarsely ground pepper

1½ teaspoons garlic powder

1½ teaspoons granulated sugar

Preheat the oven to 425°F.

Rinse the brussels sprouts and cut each of them in half. Toss the sprouts in a bowl with the rest of the ingredients until they are well coated.

Place the seasoned brussels sprouts on an ungreased baking sheet and roast in the oven for 45 to 60 minutes, rotating and flipping them occasionally. The cooking times will vary based on the oven, and convection ovens will cook quicker. Remove when a dark brown color is achieved.

Roasted Vegetables

{ S E R V E S 4 T O 6 }

This recipe makes a great side dish, and leftovers can make a healthy midday snack. At Kerber's Farm, we roast the vegetables until they slightly caramelize, which brings out the natural sweetness they possess.

Preheat the oven to 375°F.

Peel the beets and yams. Chop all the vegetables into approximately 1-inch pieces and toss with the oil and remaining ingredients.

Spread the vegetables on an ungreased baking sheet.

Cook in the oven for approximately 45 minutes, until the vegetables are brown and tender, turning every 15 minutes.

3 large beets

2 yams

1 red pepper, cored and seeded

1 yellow pepper, cored and seeded

1 zucchini

2 medium carrots, peeled

½ cup vegetable oil

1 teaspoon salt

1 teaspoon pepper

1 teaspoon granulated sugar

1 teaspoon garlic powder

Roasted Mushrooms

{ S E R V E S 4 }

This is a simple recipe that can be served as a side dish, over a salad,
or even as a meal itself. Mushrooms are a great source of
protein and can easily be integrated into most meals. Save any leftovers
and add them to an omelet with the cheese of your choice.
Mushrooms can also be simmered on the stovetop in 2 cups of
chicken stock in an uncovered pot for 15 to 20 minutes.

8 cups assorted wild mushrooms, sliced

½ cup extra virgin olive oil

2 tablespoons chopped parsley leaves

2 garlic cloves, finely chopped

1 teaspoon salt

1 teaspoon pepper

1 teaspoon granulated sugar

Preheat the oven to 400°F.

Toss all ingredients in a bowl until the mushrooms are thoroughly coated with oil and seasonings.

Spread the mushrooms on an ungreased baking sheet.

Cook in the oven for approximately 15 minutes, or until the mushrooms are tender. Cook longer if browning is desired.

TYPES OF MUSHROOMS

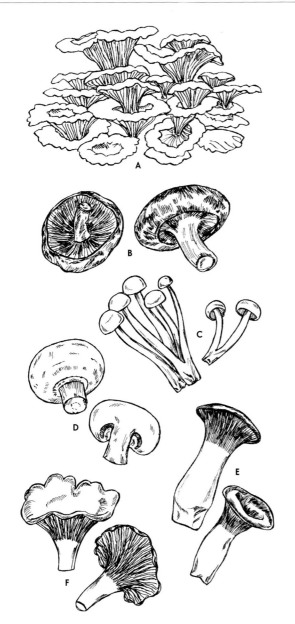

If picking wild mushrooms, you must always verify the species and confirm they are safe to consume.

A. OYSTER: These mushrooms can be found in the wild growing on trees. They are very thick and meaty, particularly around the stem.

B. SHIITAKE: These mushrooms originated in Japan and are therefore used often in Japanese cooking. They have a woodsy flavor profile and are sometimes sold dried.

C. SHIMEJI: Also known as beech mushrooms, these have a sprout-like appearance and become sweet and crunchy when cooked.

D. CHAMPIGNON: These are the most common mushrooms available. Also known as button mushrooms, they are quite mild compared to other species.

E. TRUMPET: These mushrooms grow year-round in the West and are available midsummer in the Midwest and East. They have a rich and smoky flavor.

F. CHANTERELLE: These mushrooms are known to be difficult to cultivate and are usually foraged in the wild. They have a wavy top and a thick and fleshy consistency.

Apple Cider Pork Chops with Pear Sauce

{ SERVES 4 }

This nourishing fall dish contains all of the flavors of the season, including apple cider, pears, and cloves. We often serve it with a simple salad and baked yams.

FOR THE PORK CHOPS:

2 cups apple cider

¼ teaspoon salt

¼ teaspoon pepper

4 bone-in center-cut pork chops

2 tablespoons (¼ stick) salted butter, for cooking

FOR THE PEAR SAUCE:

4 tablespoons (½ stick) salted butter

2 pears, cored and cut into ½-inch-thick slices

2 teaspoons all-purpose flour

½ cup chicken stock

6 whole cloves

¼ teaspoon salt

¼ teaspoon pepper

To make the pork chops, combine the apple cider, salt, and pepper in a medium casserole pan or deep dish. Place the pork chops in the mixture, ensuring that all of the meat is submerged. Cover and refrigerate for two hours.

To make the sauce, melt the butter in a medium saucepan on medium heat. Add the pears and cook until tender. Add the flour and gently turn the pears, taking care that they don't break. Add the chicken stock, cloves, salt, and pepper. Remove the pork chops from the cider and pour the cider into the pear mixture. Allow it to come to a boil, and then reduce to a simmer.

In a large skillet, melt 2 tablespoons butter on medium-high heat and cook the pork chops 3 to 4 minutes per side or until cooked through.

Plate the pork chops and generously ladle the pear sauce on top, removing any cloves.

Chicken Thighs with Oyster Mushrooms and Scallions

{ S E R V E S 4 }

I am likely in the minority, but my favorite part of the chicken has always
been the thigh. To me, dark meat is much more flavorful and tender than breast meat.
This dish can be made in just a few minutes. It was something I came up with
in college when I was first introduced to oyster mushrooms. With the ease of boneless,
skinless cuts, preparation is a breeze. Since the thigh is relatively small, you may
want to consider doubling this recipe for big eaters.

Place ⅓ cup of the flour on a plate. Dip each chicken
thigh in the flour, coating completely. In a large frying pan
on medium heat, melt 2 tablespoons of the butter. Add
the chicken thighs to the pan and brown on both sides,
not fully cooking them. Remove the thighs from the pan
and set aside.

Add the remaining 1 tablespoon butter to the same pan
and let it melt. Add the scallions and sauté until they are
slightly browned. Sprinkle the remaining 1 tablespoon
flour onto the scallions and mix well. Add the chicken
stock, Marsala wine, mushrooms, salt, and pepper and
bring to a simmer. Mix thoroughly to dissolve the flour.

Once simmering begins, reduce the heat to low and return
the chicken to the pan. Continue to cook for 10 to 15
minutes, or until the chicken is cooked through.

⅓ cup plus 1 tablespoon
all-purpose flour

4 boneless, skinless
chicken thighs

3 tablespoons
salted butter

⅓ cup chopped scallions

1 cup chicken stock

¼ cup Marsala wine

½ pound oyster
mushrooms

¼ teaspoon salt

¼ teaspoon pepper

WINTER

THIS TIME OF YEAR CALLS FOR QUIET NIGHTS AT HOME, GLOWING fireplaces, and knitted sweaters. The colder temperatures and shorter days allow for lots of time spent indoors, especially in the kitchen. The wonderful aroma of something simmering on the stove all day can be especially nurturing. Our winter recipes are definitely of the "feel-good" or "comfort" category. Featured in this section are warm and satisfying dishes such as mac and cheese, chili, and chicken pot pie. You will also find wintery treats such as homemade hot cocoa, fudgey brownies, and nostalgic spritz cookies.

The winter is also when we spend a lot of time in the kitchen canning and jarring jams and vegetables. We have two commercial kitchens on the property that we use for making jam, cooking maple syrup, and creating many of our packaged food products. Each winter we experiment with different ingredients and come up with tasty new products for the following year. Each item we produce is made in small batches and then assembled into gift crates or placed on the shelves in the store for sale. We also ship these handmade items to customers and other stores all around the country.

Other winter projects around the farm include lots of garden planning for the spring. We usually sketch out our ideas for layout, and we research new seed types and plant varieties. We also end up with extra beeswax after harvesting the honey in the fall. We don't want to waste this precious commodity, so several years ago we decided to create a line of all-natural homemade candles. We set up a small workshop in one of the barns and equipped it with a large wax melter and all of the tools needed to pour candles. We boil the beeswax in water to filter out debris, and then blend it with soy wax. We have experimented with different essential oils to come up with really wonderful scents. (We decided in the beginning that we would not use any of the artificial fragrances that most candles contain.)

Winter seems like it would be a quiet time of the year for a farm, but things are very different at Kerber's. Although there is a slight reprieve just after the New Year, things are still very busy all twelve months of the year. Our retail store is open year-round and very active, and our two vacation cottages are almost always booked. In addition to hosting guests and our customers, many students also visit Kerber's Farm for internships or to fulfill the community service requirements that many schools have introduced. We love working with students; we even have a farming education school planned for 2020.

WINTER RECIPES

Gluten-Free Brownies

{ MAKES 12 BROWNIES }

These thick and rich brownies are so decadent you would never believe they are gluten free. Their perfectly chewy and fudge-like consistency, coupled with a deep chocolate taste, make them one of our best-selling items. They are great served either chilled or warm and accompanied by a scoop of vanilla ice cream.

4 cups light brown sugar

6 eggs

2 teaspoons vanilla extract

24 tablespoons (3 sticks) unsalted butter

12 ounces dark chocolate, chopped

1¼ cups cornstarch

1 tablespoon xanthan gum

1¼ cups cocoa powder

¼ teaspoon salt

Preheat the oven to 350°F. Line a shallow 9-by-13-inch pan with foil and spray with baking spray.

In a stand mixer fitted with a paddle attachment, combine the sugar, eggs, and vanilla and mix on medium speed until light in color.

While the sugar and eggs are mixing, melt the butter in a small saucepan. Place the chocolate in a medium bowl. Once the butter is completely melted, pour it over the chocolate and let it sit for 2 minutes. Mix the chocolate and butter using a rubber spatula until the chocolate has completely melted.

In a small bowl, sift together the cornstarch, xanthan gum, cocoa powder, and salt. Set aside.

With the mixer running on low, slowly add the melted chocolate. Continue to mix as you slowly add the dry ingredients. Mix until just combined.

Pour the batter into the prepared pan and bake for 30 to 35 minutes. The brownies are done when a knife comes out slightly crumby (it will not be clean, which is OK; these brownies are intensely fudgey). Let the brownies cool to room temperature before cutting.

Linzer Tarts

{ MAKES APPROXIMATELY 12 COOKIES }

Originating in Austria in cake form as a Linzer torte, these decadent treats are a cookie adaptation made with ground almonds and a shortbread-like dough. Our version is light and buttery, and we line them with our Kerberry Jam, although any flavor of jam will work.

Preheat the oven to 350°F.

Spread the almonds on a baking sheet, and then toast them for 5 to 7 minutes; keep the oven on. Let the almonds cool, and then grind them in a food processor.

In a small bowl, combine the ground almonds, flour, and cinnamon. Whisk together.

In a stand mixer fitted with a paddle attachment, add the butter and sugar. Mix on medium speed until light and fluffy. With the mixer running on low speed, slowly add the flour mixture until combined.

On a floured surface, roll the dough to a ⅛-inch thickness and cut out as many cookies as possible with the 3-inch cutter. Half will be the tops and half will be the bottoms. For the tops of the cookies, cut out the centers using the smaller cutter. Reroll the scraps and cut out more cookies. Place the cookies on a baking sheet coated with baking spray and place in the refrigerator for 15 minutes.

Bake the cookies for 15 minutes or until lightly golden, and then let cool. Once cooled, take the bottom halves of the cookies and spread about 1 teaspoon of jam on each. Cover the top halves completely with the sifted powdered sugar. Place the tops of the cookies onto the bottoms.

1¼ cups sliced almonds

1½ cups all-purpose flour

1 teaspoon ground cinnamon

16 tablespoons (2 sticks) unsalted butter, softened

½ cup granulated sugar

½ cup Kerberry Jam (see page 94)

½ cup powdered sugar, sifted

SPECIAL EQUIPMENT:

3-inch cookie cutter

2-inch cookie cutter

Hot Cocoa

{ S E R V E S 4 }

Nothing is better on a snowy winter's day than steaming hot cocoa
topped with rich whipped cream. And it's even better when made with milk
instead of water. The dry mix for this recipe can be made in bulk,
stored in the pantry, and then used when desired. Some small chocolate
chips will remain in the beverage as an added surprise.

4 cups whole milk

½ cup cocoa powder

¾ cup granulated sugar

¼ cup mini dark
chocolate chips

Pinch of salt

Whipped cream, for
topping (see page 133)

Marshmallows, for
topping (optional)

Bring the milk to a simmer in a medium saucepan on
medium-high heat. In a small bowl, combine the cocoa
powder, sugar, chocolate chips, and salt and stir together.
Add ½ cup of the hot cocoa mix to the milk and stir
until the chocolate has melted. Serve immediately in
a mug topped with whipped cream and, if desired,
marshmallows. Store the remaining chocolate mix in a
12-ounce jar to use in the future.

CANDLEMAKING

I have always been mesmerized by the flickering flame of a candle, and I learned how to make them in a junior high art class. This first candle was quite crude: paraffin wax melted with red dye, mixed with a holiday fragrance, and then poured into a Styrofoam cup. But as simple as it was, I was hooked on the art of making my own candles.

During the cold days of winter during college, I remember going to a craft store and buying the supplies needed to make candles in my dorm room. I would make five or six at a time and give them to my friends as gifts. The soothing flame would bring a certain warmth and coziness to my room, one that only a candle or fireplace can bring.

When I bought Kerber's Farm, I immediately knew I wanted to get back into candlemaking. The abundance of rambling barns gave me plenty of space to set up a studio, and I began to experiment with using different waxes and fragrances. I have since developed a line of clean-burning, all-natural candles that are made with soy wax, beeswax, and pure essential oils. Below is an easy-to-follow recipe that you can try at home.

HOMEMADE CANDLES · *Makes 6 candles*

Metal pouring pitcher or old pot

4 pounds soy wax (blend with beeswax if desired)

6 (6-inch) wicks

6 (8-ounce) glass jars

Double-sided tape dots

6 popsicle sticks

4 to 6 ounces essential oils (mix varieties as desired)

Instant-read thermometer

In an old pot or wax-melting pitcher, melt the wax over medium heat. While it is melting, adhere the wick bases to the bottoms of the jars with tape dots. Center the wicks upright by laying a notched popsicle stick across the top of each jar. Once the wax has melted, remove it from the heat and allow it to cool to 120°F, using the thermometer to check. Add the essential oils and mix well, trying not to create bubbles. Carefully pour the wax into each jar, leaving approximately ½ inch of space at the top. Allow it to cool until completely hardened (approximately 4 hours). Remove the popsicle sticks and cut the wicks to ¾ inch above the top of the wax surface.

Spritz Cookies

{ MAKES 3½ DOZEN COOKIES }

These cookies originated in Germany, and the word "spritz" means to inject or squirt—the dough is pushed through a cookie press. Spritz cookies were always a holiday tradition at my house when I was growing up, and my mother used a vintage aluminum cookie press. I can still remember the taste of the raw buttery and sweet cookie dough that was left over. I knew I wanted to feature these cookies at Kerber's Farm at the holidays, and they have been very popular.

Place a clean, dry, ungreased baking sheet in the freezer. Preheat the oven to 350°F.

In a stand mixer fitted with a paddle attachment, add the butter and sugar. Mix on medium speed until light and fluffy, 2 to 3 minutes. Stop the mixer and scrape down the sides and bottom of the bowl with a rubber spatula. Turn the mixer on medium-low speed and add the yolks and vanilla. Continue mixing as you slowly add the flour and then the salt. Mix until the dough just comes together.

Fill the cookie gun with the dough. Take the baking sheet out of the freezer. Holding the gun at a 90-degree angle while touching the pan, press the trigger and lift straight up (this may take three or four presses depending on how full the gun is). The cookie should stick to the cold pan. Continue to press cookies onto the baking sheet until no dough remains. Bake the cookies for 12 to 15 minutes, or until golden brown.

8 tablespoons (1 stick) unsalted butter, softened

½ cup granulated sugar

2 egg yolks

½ teaspoon vanilla extract

1 cup all-purpose flour

⅛ teaspoon salt

1 tablespoon colored crystal sugar, for topping

SPECIAL EQUIPMENT:

Cookie gun

Buttermilk Waffles or Pancakes

This is always a favorite breakfast dish when I host my friends in one of the guesthouses at Kerber's Farm. Even my healthiest, non-carbohydrate-eating friends cannot resist these fluffy treats—particularly when topped with warm butter, berries, and pure maple syrup. This recipe works for both waffles and pancakes, and you may substitute wheat flour if desired.

2 cups all-purpose flour

4 tablespoons granulated sugar

2 teaspoons baking soda

Pinch of salt

2 eggs

2 cups buttermilk

Add all the dry ingredients to a medium bowl and mix. In a separate bowl, whisk together the eggs and buttermilk. Pour the buttermilk mixture into the dry ingredients and whisk.

If making waffles, preheat a waffle iron on medium heat and coat the cooking surfaces with baking spray. Pour approximately ⅓ cup of the batter onto the center of the bottom griddle and close the lid. Cook for 1 to 2 minutes, until golden brown. Repeat until all the batter is used.

If making pancakes, preheat a pan or griddle on medium heat and coat with baking spray. Pour approximately ⅓ cup of the batter into the pan for each pancake, making as many pancakes as will fit without touching. Cook for approximately 2 minutes per side.

Serve with fresh berries, butter, maple syrup, or jam.

Mac and Cheese Pie

{ MAKES ONE 9-INCH PIE }

Our take on macaroni and cheese is a bit different. In keeping with Kerber's tradition, we have adapted this dish to be a "pie" that can be served as a meal alongside a simple salad or vegetable. We crumble our hearty cheddar buttermilk biscuits to form a crust-like base to the pie. Meat lovers may also mix chopped bacon or pancetta into the macaroni.

¼ cup plus ¾ teaspoon salt

¼ cup olive oil

¾ pound orecchiette pasta

6 ounces shredded mozzarella cheese

4 ounces shredded white cheddar cheese

5 ounces shredded provolone cheese

4 tablespoons (½ stick) unsalted butter

4½ teaspoons all-purpose flour

¾ cup whole milk

1⅓ cups heavy cream

1¼ teaspoons granulated sugar

½ teaspoon Frank's hot sauce

Pinch of ground white pepper

1 cheddar buttermilk biscuit (see page 62)

In a medium pot, bring 1 gallon of water to a rolling boil. Once the water is boiling, add ¼ cup salt and the oil, and then the orecchiette. Cook the pasta for 10 minutes, until al dente. Drain and set the pasta aside.

In a small bowl, mix all three cheeses together. Separate into two equal batches and set aside.

In a medium pot over low to medium heat, melt the butter. Once melted, add the flour and whisk together. Once combined, while whisking, slowly add the milk and heavy cream until fully incorporated. Add the remaining ¾ teaspoon salt, the sugar, hot sauce, and white pepper. Continue to mix every so often until the milk is hot. Once hot, slowly add one batch of the cheese and continue whisking until the cheeses have melted completely. Remove the pot from the heat.

Add the cooked pasta to the cheese sauce and mix until completely coated. Let the pasta and cheese mixture chill in the refrigerator for 1 to 2 hours.

Preheat the oven to 350°F. Break or chop the biscuit into small pieces. Place the pieces on a baking sheet and toast for 5 to 8 minutes.

Add the toasted biscuit pieces to a 9-inch pie plate. Add half of the remaining batch of cheese to the top of the

biscuits. Pour the chilled mac and cheese filling into the
pie plate, spreading evenly with a slight peak in the center.
Cover completely with the remaining cheese.

Place the pie plate on a baking sheet and bake for 20 to 25
minutes, until the cheese on top is golden brown.

Dinner Rolls

{ MAKES 12 ROLLS }

This is a foolproof and simple recipe for warm, delicious dinner rolls.
At Kerber's Farm, we use these rolls for many of our lunch sandwiches and also serve
them with meals. They are great served warm with a pat of butter, which seems to
accentuate the subtle and delicate flavors of the yeast, salt, and sugar.

4½ teaspoons active dry yeast

¼ cup granulated sugar

2 teaspoons salt

6 cups all-purpose flour

2 teaspoons vegetable oil

1 egg, for wash

In a stand mixer fitted with a dough hook attachment, add 2 cups of lukewarm water, the yeast, and the sugar. Let stand for approximately 5 minutes until creamy.

Turn the mixer on medium-low speed and add the salt. Slowly add the flour and continue to mix for approximately 5 more minutes or until the dough is smooth to the touch and no longer sticky.

Take a medium bowl and coat completely with the oil (or spray with baking spray). Remove the dough from the mixer and place it in the bowl. Cover it with plastic wrap or a damp kitchen towel and let it rise for 1 hour. Remove the cover and pat the dough down gently with your hands to release excess air.

Preheat the oven to 350°F. In a small bowl, mix together the egg and 1 tablespoon of water. Set aside. Line a baking sheet with parchment paper.

Place the dough onto a lightly floured surface and cut into 12 equal pieces. Roll each piece into a ball and place on the prepared baking sheet. Brush with the egg wash and bake for 20 to 25 minutes, until the rolls are lightly golden brown.

Potato Pancakes

{ MAKES APPROXIMATELY 12 PANCAKES }

My grandfather emigrated from Greece to the United States when he was 15 years old. He started working as a dishwasher and eventually owned a string of successful diners in New York City. This dish is based on his recipe, which my mother often made for me as a child. I hope you share it with your family as well.

2 eggs

3 large potatoes

¼ cup chopped onion

¼ cup milk

2 teaspoons baking powder

2 tablespoons chopped parsley leaves

1½ teaspoons salt

1½ teaspoons pepper

1½ cups all-purpose flour

4 cups vegetable oil, for frying

1 cup applesauce

SPECIAL EQUIPMENT:

Candy thermometer

Beat the eggs in a small bowl. Set aside.

Rinse and peel the potatoes. Using a box grater, shred the potatoes and place them in a medium bowl. Add the eggs, onion, milk, baking powder, parsley, salt, and pepper and combine well. Add the flour and mix.

In a large frying pan on medium to high heat, heat the oil to approximately 350°F. Using your hands, scoop out and form the mixture into a 2-inch ball and squeeze out any excess liquid. Flatten the ball with your hands to form a pancake and then gently slide it into the hot oil, taking care not to splash. Cook 5 or 6 pancakes at a time, or whatever amount fits across the bottom of the pan.

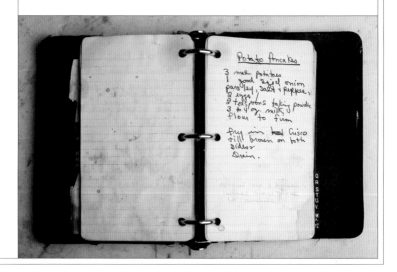

Cook for a few minutes per side, until golden brown. Place
the cooked pancakes on paper towels to absorb excess oil.
Repeat the cooking process until all of the mixture is used.
Serve the pancakes warm with applesauce.

Braised Chicken with Root Vegetables and Apples

{ SERVES 4 }

In the fall and winter, I love to make use of a heavy cast-iron Dutch oven
to make wholesome one-pot meals. The simplicity of browning the meat in the pot
and then using the drippings as a basis to build on the dish always appeals
to me. The chicken in this easy-to-make recipe could be replaced with pork butt,
short ribs, or any other meat you desire with varied cooking times.

4 celery stalks

2 large carrots, peeled

2 large parsnips, peeled

2 apples

1 medium onion

1 tablespoon salted
butter

1 whole chicken, rinsed

½ teaspoon salt

½ teaspoon pepper

2 cups chicken stock

Pinch of granulated
sugar

SPECIAL EQUIPMENT:

Instant-read
thermometer

Preheat the oven to 350°F.

Cut the celery, carrots, and parsnips into 2-inch pieces.
Cut the apples into ½-inch wedges, as you would for
an apple pie. Chop the onion into a fine dice. Put the
ingredients aside, keeping the onions separate.

In a 6- to 8-quart Dutch oven, melt the butter on
medium-high heat. Coat the entire outside of the chicken
with salt and pepper, and place it in the pot once the
butter has melted. Brown each side, 4 to 5 minutes per
side. Remove the chicken from the pot.

With the heat on medium, add the onions and
brown them. Return the chicken to the pot with the
onions and then add the chicken stock, sugar, and
the rest of the vegetables.

Place the covered pot in the oven for approximately
1 hour, basting the chicken occasionally. After 1 hour,
remove the cover and cook for another 30 to 45
minutes, or until the thigh meat reaches 165°F on an
instant-read thermometer.

Let the chicken rest for approximately 20 minutes
before serving.

TYPES OF
ROOT VEGGIES

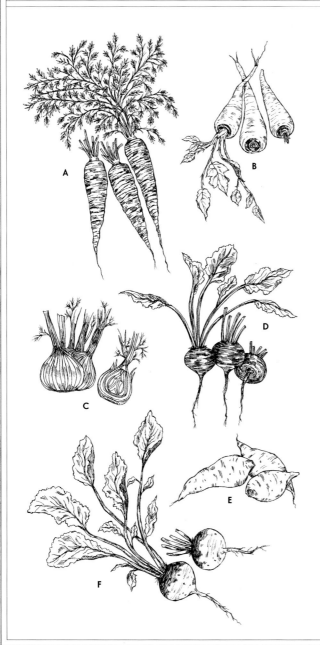

Grown mostly underground, these hearty and durable vegetables can be stored for months at a time in a cool, dark place.

A. CARROTS: Carrots are crisp and naturally sweet. Using them in soups and sauces is a great way to avoid having to add refined sugar.

B. PARSNIPS: White in color, these vegetables have a cinnamon-like flavor. They are great for roasting, braising, or puréeing.

C. FENNEL: These vegetables are shorter than celery and have large white bulbs at the bottom. Fennel has a licorice flavor and can be chopped up raw and used in salads or roasted.

D. BEETS: Beets are high in beta-carotene and antioxidants. They are commonly steamed to soften their texture, but can also be eaten raw.

E. YAMS: These vegetables are delicious mashed or puréed. Their natural sweetness makes them great in soups, muffins, cookies, or breads.

F. TURNIPS: These very hard and dense root vegetables make a great side dish when mashed and mixed with butter and a little cream.

Carrot and Chicken Soup

{ S E R V E S 5 }

Our healthy and hearty carrot and chicken soup is a great source of
vitamins and protein. This is, hands down, the most popular soup we have ever
served at Kerber's Farm. The puréed carrots create a wonderful
thick texture that suspends the chicken and other ingredients.

2 boneless chicken
breasts

2 tablespoons vegetable
oil

1 teaspoon pepper

1 teaspoon plus 1
tablespoon salt

6 carrots, washed,
peeled, and chopped
into 2-inch chunks

2 tablespoons (¼ stick)
unsalted butter

½ cup diced celery

½ cup diced onion

1½ cups chicken broth

1 tablespoon chopped
parsley leaves

Preheat the oven to 350°F.

In a medium bowl, add the chicken breasts, oil, pepper,
and 1 teaspoon salt. Mix until coated completely. Place the
chicken on a baking sheet and bake for 20 to 25 minutes,
until completely cooked through. Set aside.

In a medium pot on high heat, add 8 cups of water and
the carrots and bring to a boil. Cook until the carrots are
tender, 10 to 15 minutes. Slowly add the carrots and water
to a food processor or blender and purée or blend until
completely smooth. (Or, if using a stick blender, place it
directly in the pot and blend until no chunks remain.)
Return the carrot purée to the pot and reduce to low heat.

In a small frying pan over medium heat, melt the butter
and add the celery and onions. Cook until the onions are
translucent, approximately 5 minutes. Add the onions and
celery to the carrot purée.

Next, add the chicken broth, the remaining 1 tablespoon salt,
and the parsley leaves. Last, chop the cooked chicken into
½-inch pieces and add to the soup. Allow to simmer for 10
to 15 minutes and then serve.

Beef Chili

{ SERVES 5 TO 6 }

This hearty wintertime favorite is easy to make and a great meal to let simmer on the stove on a cold winter's day. It goes well with rice, quinoa, or lentils. For a vegan option, substitute vegetable broth and meatless crumbles for the beef stock and beef.

In a medium pot, heat the oil over medium heat. Add the carrots, onions, celery, and bell peppers and cook for 5 minutes, until the onions are translucent.

Add the beef to the pot with the vegetables and cook through, about 5 minutes.

Add the kidney beans, beef stock, tomato paste, oregano, garlic powder, chili powder, sugar, pepper, and Cajun spice and stir. Bring to a boil and then reduce the heat to low and simmer for 20 minutes. Add the parsley. Garnish with sour cream and cheese and serve.

1 tablespoon olive oil

½ cup diced carrots

½ cup diced onion

½ cup diced celery

½ cup diced yellow bell pepper

½ cup diced red bell pepper

1 pound ground beef (85% lean)

1 (16-ounce) can red kidney beans

2 cups beef stock

¼ cup tomato paste

2 teaspoons dried oregano

4½ teaspoons garlic powder

4½ teaspoons chili powder

2 tablespoons granulated sugar

2 teaspoons pepper

2 teaspoons Cajun spice

1 tablespoon chopped parsley leaves

Sour cream, for garnish

Shredded jack cheese, for garnish

Chicken Pot Pie

{ MAKES ONE 9-INCH PIE }

Kerber's Farm was originally a poultry farm, and one of its best-selling items was chicken pot pie. When I purchased Kerber's in 2013, I wanted to honor this heritage and continue the legacy by reimagining this popular dish. This decadent and rich comfort food is sure to please, and it has been voted the "tastiest dish" by Taste of Long Island.

2 boneless chicken breasts

2 tablespoons olive oil

1 teaspoon pepper, plus more for topping

2½ teaspoons salt, plus more for topping

¾ pound Yukon Gold potatoes, chopped into 1-inch pieces

5 tablespoons unsalted butter

1¼ cups diced onions

¾ cup all-purpose flour, plus more for rolling out

¾ cup heavy cream

¼ cup chicken stock

1 tablespoon granulated sugar

½ cup frozen carrot and pea mix

1 tablespoon chopped parsley leaves

1 tablespoon chopped sage

1 egg, for wash

1 pie crust dough (see page 52)

Preheat the oven to 350°F.

In a medium bowl, add the chicken breasts, oil, pepper, and 1 teaspoon of the salt. Mix and coat completely. Place the chicken on a baking sheet and bake for 20 to 25 minutes, until completely cooked through. Set aside. Turn off oven.

Do not peel the potatoes. While the chicken is cooking, add the potatoes to a medium pot and fill with water until they are covered by 1 inch of water. Bring to a boil over medium heat and cook until tender. Once the potatoes are cooked, drain the water completely and set them aside to cool while you make the rest of the filling.

In a saucepan on medium heat, melt the butter. Add the onions and cook until translucent, approximately 5 minutes. Whisk the flour into the butter and onions, and then add the heavy cream and chicken stock. Continue to whisk until combined. Add the sugar, the remaining 1½ teaspoons salt, and carrot and pea mix. Mix until combined.

Remove from the heat and add the contents to a medium bowl. Add the potatoes, parsley leaves, and sage and mix. Chop the roasted chicken into 1-inch pieces and add to the bowl. Mix until combined. Let the mixture chill in the refrigerator for 1 to 2 hours.

Preheat the oven to 350°F. In a small bowl, mix together the egg and 1 tablespoon of water. Set aside.

Cut the refrigerated pie crust dough into two equal halves. Lightly dust the countertop with flour and roll out each piece of dough to a 10-inch circle that is approximately ⅛ inch thick. Carefully lift one rolled-out crust into a 9-inch pie plate and gently shape to the form of the plate. Pour the chilled chicken filling into the crust and spread evenly. Place the second half of the dough over the top of the pie, trimming any excess dough that hangs over. Tuck and crimp the edges along the perimeter of the pie crust. If desired, the excess dough can be rolled out, cut into a shape with a cookie cutter, and then placed on top for decoration (we use a rooster).

Brush the top of the crust with the egg wash and place the rooster cutout (if using) on top. Also brush the cutout with the egg wash. Lightly sprinkle salt and pepper over the pie.

Place the pie on a baking sheet and set it in the oven. Bake for 25 to 30 minutes, and then cover the pie with foil and continue baking for an additional 20 minutes. Let the pie rest for 5 to 10 minutes and then serve.

Gluten-Free Berry Oat Dog Biscuits

{ MAKES 24 BISCUITS }

I first created this recipe many years ago for my English Labrador, Charlie. She loved them so much that I decided to sell them at the store. They are very healthy, with simple, wholesome ingredients and no added sugar. The biscuits will keep in the fridge for up to two weeks or freeze in plastic for up to three months.

1 cup blueberries

1 cup raspberries

2 cups rolled oats

2 cups gluten-free flour

Preheat the oven to 350°F. Line a baking sheet with parchment paper or foil.

Place all ingredients in a food processor and blend until everything is combined. On a lightly floured surface, roll the dough to a ½-inch thickness and cut out the biscuits with your desired cutter (we use a dog bone shape). Place the biscuits on the prepared baking sheet.

Bake for 20 to 25 minutes, until lightly golden on the edges.

ACCOMMODATIONS

Only an hour from New York City, Kerber's Farm encourages its guests to explore the property, unwind, and immerse themselves in the farming lifestyle. To help with this, Kerber's offers two nautically inspired guesthouses for overnight visits and extended stays. Each home has been carefully restored with beautiful finishes and modern conveniences.

The Captain's Cottage is a one-bedroom cabin that features a queen-sized bed, a living room with a fireplace, and a full kitchen with marble countertops. There are also additional sleeping accommodations in a loft that is accessible via a vintage library ladder.

The Farm House is a private three-bedroom home that has a charming living room with exposed beams, a fireplace, and a baby grand piano. There is also a full chef's kitchen with stainless-steel appliances.

✻ ACKNOWLEDGMENTS ✻

Having the chance to write a book about a farm that I saved from being destroyed is truly a gift. Ever since I was a young boy growing up on Long Island, Kerber's Farm has had a special place in my heart. Seeing it thrive and its legacy now immortalized in this book brings me enormous pleasure.

I'd like to thank the Kerber family, who founded the farm, for their support and input. Particularly, I'd like to thank Arthur Kerber for contributing all of the historical photos found in this book.

At Kerber's Farm, I'd like to thank my dedicated team, particularly Bonnie Boriotto, Devin Dowd, Mimi Ewald, and Ivy Soric. Their devotion is unparalleled, and they run the business as if it were their own.

I'd like to thank Lindsay Morris for photographing this book. We had a lot of fun over the past year or so doing everything from cooking and sailing to clamming and playing with the chickens—all to get the perfect shot. I'd also like to thank Doug Young for contributing additional photographs and Robin Diamond for her wonderful illustrations.

At Rizzoli I'd like to thank my publishers Charles Miers and James Muschett for once again giving me the incredible opportunity to write a book with this iconic publishing house. I am grateful for their trust and support.

Also at Rizzoli I'd like to thank my editor, Candice Fehrman, whose finesse and style always complements my words. I'd like to acknowledge Pam Sommers and Jessica Napp for the enormous amount of work they do in promoting these projects. I'd like to thank designer Susi Oberhelman for her incredible eye in the design of this book and its beautiful cover. Thank you also to my literary agent Carla Glasser, who continues to have great faith in my work.

I'd like to thank a group of my friends who have pitched in through the years with physical labor at the farm: Brian Carmody, Jared Craft, Robert Hammond, Barry Jordan, Scott Lawrie, Rob Levy, Murdoch Mackinnon, Charlie McMillen, Jake Milnor, Chris Peregrin, Lisle Richards, Andrew Salmen, Andrew Taylor, and my brother Chris Voulgaris.

I am grateful to my parents for giving me a childhood that included Kerber's Farm. They have been a great source of support through the years.

Last, I'd like to thank the many customers who believe in what we are doing at Kerber's Farm and the countless strangers who have written me personal notes thanking me for saving it. Places like Kerber's Farm help make small communities even greater.

ABOUT THE CONTRIBUTORS

NICK VOULGARIS III purchased Kerber's Farm in 2013 and saved it from being developed into condominiums. He had frequented the farm and its country store as a child and wanted to preserve its legacy. Nick is passionate about cooking and loves to entertain. He is the author of Rizzoli's *Coffee from A to Z*, *The Seaside House*, *Chris-Craft Boats*, and *Hinkley Yachts*. He lives in Manhattan and, in the summer, aboard his classic Alden ketch in Sag Harbor, New York.

LINDSAY MORRIS is photo editor of *Edible Magazine*. Her work has been featured on BBC World News and published in *Time*, *New York Magazine*, *The New York Times Magazine*, *Scientific American*, *GEO*, and *Vanity Fair*. She has recently published her first monograph with Kehrer Verlag, *You Are You*, documenting a summer camp for gender-creative children and their families. She resides on the East End of Long Island with her husband, two sons, chickens, and a cat named Blue.

ROBIN DIAMOND is an artist and illustrator based in Oyster Bay, New York. Her illustrations, watercolors, and portraits have appeared in the J. Peterman catalog and she has worked with a variety of other retailers, including Banana Republic, Victoria's Secret, Ralph Lauren, and Calvin Klein.